ACL Soda Bottles of Rhode Island

TAYLOR McBURNEY

ACL Soda Bottles of Rhode Island

Copyright © 2022 Taylor McBurney

Produced and printed by Stillwater River Publications. All rights reserved. Written and produced in the United States of America. This book may not be reproduced or sold in any form without the expressed, written permission of the author and publisher.

Visit our website at
www.StillwaterPress.com
for more information.

First Stillwater River Publications Edition

ISBN: 978-1-958217-29-0

Library of Congress Control Number: 2022911734

1 2 3 4 5 6 7 8 9 10

Written by Taylor McBurney.
Published by Stillwater River Publications,
Pawtucket, RI, USA.

Names: McBurney, Taylor, author.
Title: Rhode Island ACL soda bottles / Taylor McBurney.
Description: First Stillwater River Publications edition. | Pawtucket, RI, USA : Stillwater River Publications, [2022]
Identifiers: ISBN: 978-1-958217-29-0 | LCCN: 2022911734
Subjects: LCSH: Soft drinks--Labeling--Rhode Island--Pictorial works. | Beverages--Packaging--Rhode Island--Pictorial works. | Bottles--Collectibles--Rhode Island--Pictorial works. | Soft drink industry--Rhode Island--History--20th century--Pictorial works. | Bottle industry--Rhode Island--History--20th century--Pictorial works. |
LCGFT: Illustrated works.
Classification: LCC: TP659 .M32 2022 | DDC: 663/.62--dc23

*The views and opinions expressed
in this book are solely those of the author
and do not necessarily reflect the views
and opinions of the publisher.*

In memory of Joseph Prentiss.

Contents

Acknowledgments vii

1. A Brief History of ACL Soda Bottles 1
2. Dating ACL Soda Bottles 3
3. Key for Reading ACL Descriptions 4
4. RI ACL Soda Bottle Company Histories 6
5. RI ACL Sodas List 20

Acknowledgments

This book was first proposed by club member Al Otis sometime around 2011. Significant progress was made in assembling a list of all of the known Rhode Island ACL sodas, but ultimately Al decided not to pursue the creation and publication of a book. However, I was inspired by his efforts and decided to do my best to bring them to fruition. It may have taken me over 10 years to finally get around to it, but here it is!

I would like to thank everyone who helped contribute to this book, as I certainly would not have been able to do it on my own! Key contributors include Al Otis, Tom Mendes, Bob Lampher, and Art Pawlowski. Each of them contributed many hours to this endeavor providing pictures and information on different bottles.

I would also like to thank the following collectors, pickers, and diggers for their valuable contributions as well!

David Curenton
Leona Brown
Karsten Kydland
Christopher Weide
John McCoy
Mike from Pawtucket
David Gates

David Smith
Hank Pendleton
Steve Carter
Ed Greer
Joe DeFeo
Vinny Fava
Carl Tourgee

Joseph Prentiss
Ryan Berlin
Patrick Harnedy
Josh Joutras
Timothy B. Miller
John Sgambato

A Brief History of ACL Soda Bottles

For those not familiar with the term, ACL stands for applied color label. They can go by other names including pyroglaze (commonly used to described milk bottles with this type of label), painted label, or the similar process of enameling.

While embossing was enough to identify the contents and owner of a bottle, it could never be as colorful as a paper label. The problem was that almost all soda bottles were re-used many times during their life span. A paper label would simply be washed off during the cleaning and sterilization cycle. This re-labeling process was not only a headache for bottlers but also cut into their profits. Luckily by the 1930s a solution was on the horizon.

The first ACL soda bottle dates to around 1934. The process involved applying a paste made of ground lead, borosilicate glass, and mineral pigments to a bottle that was still hot (roughly 1,100° Fahrenheit). The process had to be repeated for each color, which made the process more expensive with each added color. This process fused a vibrantly colored label directly to the glass, allowing the bottler to wash and reuse bottles with this colorful labeling remaining fully intact. As with most innovative ideas, ACL labels were slow to catch on in the 1930s, as only a few brands have ACL bottles from this decade. However, by 1940 these labels were taking off in a big way, and by 1945 about half of the existing bottling companies were using ACLs. They reached their heyday in the late 1940s through the 1960s. In the mid-1950s a new cheaper method of applying ACL labels was developed. This also made using multiple colors much cheaper. With the introduction of the NDNR (no deposit, no return) bottles, they slowly started to loose popularity.

Plastic bottles also became big competitors as well. However, despite the competition and loss of appeal, one can still find ACL soda bottles being sold in stores today.

One can be easily confused with similar terms such as "pyroglazed" (nicknamed pyro) labels. This is what painted label milk bottles are called. While the method of applying the label is virtually the same, for some reason the term "pyroglazed" won out. If you dig for bottles, you will find that pyro milks generally do not survive as well as ACL sodas. This is probably because most ACL sodas have a slightly different composition, and the labels tended to have more solid designs with multiple colors, while pyro milks usually just have thin pyro lettering. One will also notice that the earlier pyro labels hold up better than those created using the newer method developed in the 1950s. There are also ACL medicine bottles from the 1930s-40s. These are also collectible, but not nearly as popular as sodas and milks due to their relative scarcity and obscurity.

Rhode Island was on target with most states when it came to using ACL soda bottles. The first plant to use them was the Deep Rock Co. in West Barrington, RI. Made by the Owens Illinois Glass Co., these bottles have informative date codes on the bottom of the bottle. The earliest one I have found dates to 1937.

These early bottles have single color labels (in this case red for clear bottles and yellow for green bottles). The process had not yet been perfected, so the bottles found from this era often have faded or peeling labels. The Deep Rock plant went on to bottle a number of different soda brands including Alka-Time, Dr. Swett's Root Beer, King Orange Soda, and Xtra.

Dating ACL Soda Bottles

This is perhaps one of my favorite aspects of ACL soda bottles. Unlike many bottles, virtually all of these sodas have date codes that can be found on the base, heel, or lip of the bottle. Usually it is a two number code like 47 for 1947. Other companies like Glenshaw used an alphabetic code.

Below is a list of all the known trademarks found on Rhode Island ACL sodas, and where the date code can be found:

Two number date code to the right of trademark on bottom of bottle:
Anchor Hocking Glass Co.
Illinois Glass Co.
Oil City Glass Co.
Owens-Illinois Glass Co.
Reed Glass Co.
Thatcher Glass Co.

Date code is letter on lower portion of crown top lip of bottle (often illegible):
Glenshaw Glass Co.

No known date code:
Chattanooga Glass Co.

Key for Reading ACL Descriptions

I settled on a two letter code to identify different soda brands found on RI ACL sodas. They are as follows:

AK	Alaska	**GR**	Grandpa's Draft Type N.E. Style	**RZ**	Ritz-E
AT	Alka-Time			**RO**	Rose
BA	Batchelors	**GS**	Girard Spring	**RC**	Royal Crown
BS	Berry Spring	**HE**	Hebe	**SU**	Seven-Up
BL	Brooklawn	**HC**	Hope Club	**SH**	Shiloh
BR	Bridge Club	**ID**	Ideal	**SC**	South County
BC	Brownie Club	**KR**	Kerona	**SI**	Simba
CD	Canada Dry	**KO**	King Orange Soda	**SB**	Speedball
CH	Champagner	**LA**	Lamberts	**SK**	Spike It
CL	Clover Club	**LG**	Ledge	**SP**	Spur
CC	Coca-Cola	**LC**	Liberty Club	**SQ**	Squirt
CT	Cott	**LU**	Lime-Up	**ST**	Star
CN	Cotton Club	**MN**	Manhattan	**SE**	Seacrest
DA	Daily Aid	**MR**	Martins	**SW**	Doctor Swett's
DR	Deep Rock	**MC**	Mission Club (same as Mission?)	**TC**	Town Club
DX	Dexter			**TA**	Tru-Ade
DM	Drink Me	**MI**	Mission	**TD**	Tweed
DV	Dub-L-Valu	**MH**	Moose Head	**TW**	Twin City
DY	Dybala's Spring	**NE**	Nehi	**VD**	Virginia Dare
DS	E.J. Dybala Soda	**NC**	Newport Club	**WC**	Warwick Club
EA	Eagle	**NU**	Nugget	**WL**	Wellington Club
EM	Empire/Empire Club	**OC**	Ochee	**WE**	Westerly Club
ES	Echo Spring	**OE**	Old English	**XR**	Xtra
FY	Frisky	**PC**	Pepsi-Cola	**YC**	Yacht Club
FR	Frostie Root Beer	**RF**	Red Fox	**YA**	Yankee
GC	Glee Club	**RR**	Red Rock		

How the Abbreviated System Works

Each unique brand gets its own abbreviation. Major variations within a brand (such as Clover Club Beverages, Clover Club Ginger Ale, Clover Club Sparkling Water) all have the same abbreviation. They would be designated CL-1, CL-2, and CL-3, although each version of each brand would be listed, so if Clover Club Beverages has four variants, it would take up CL-1 to 4. The same would go for brands bottled in multiple towns by different bottlers.

I will try to initially organize the known examples in a way that makes some sense (usually chronologically and capacity).

If an new variant is found after the book is published, it will simply be added as the next number (so if there were 8 Clover Club bottles listed and a new one was found it would become CL-9).

Individual Listing Key

BOTTLE FEATURES
Color (ex. Green)
Design (ex. Plain bottle, hobbleskirt, diamond pattern) (only glass design, not ACL)
Embossing (on the glass) (ex. Registered, Ochee) (not always included if there is only one variety)

Bottle manufacturer (ex. Glenshaw Glass Co.)
Date (ex. 1944)

ACL WRITING
Brand (ex. Yacht Club)
Bottler (ex. Yacht Club Bottling Works)
Capacity (ex. 12oz.)
ACL colors (ex. Red and white) (try to list dominant color first)

Motto or **slogan** (ex. It Sings in the Glass)
Key ACL design (ex. Baseball on Speedball bottle)

ADDITIONAL DISCRIMINATION
Many bottles have very minute differences in the label. Some things to note would be:

Additional writing, like zip codes, telephone numbers, or patent info.
Different writing styles, like cursive and block letters
Writing that is filled vs unfilled (unfilled writing is an ACL label with transparent letters inside it)

The location or organization of different words
How the capacity is described (one quart compared to 32 oz.)

REFERENCES
Beverage Blue Book 1925
Beverage Bureau 1927-2013

Providence Business Directory 1940-1970s
Other town business directories

RI ACL Soda Bottle Company Histories

These are the histories of bottling companies in Rhode Island that used ACL (Applied Color Label) soda bottles. Some of the brands are not listed separately but instead listed under the company that bottled them. Date ranges shown are the known dates of ACL sodas bottles from that company. The range is likely wider and will be adjusted as new dates are found.

Notes: When referring to company ownership, I came across three different titles. "Owner" means that person owned the company in its entirety. A "president" may own the company, or they might just be in charge of it (for example, if the owner is too ill or old). A "manager" is always considered to be a step below the president.

Bare Rock Beverage Company

The Bare Rock Beverage Co. was located in Graniteville, RI. Established in 1919 as the Bare Rock Spring, it was located at 250-252 Putnam Pike from 1940-1965. It was first called the Bare Rock Beverage Co. in 1940. They bottled Virginia Dare brand beverages from 1945-1965. This included Korker, a lemon lime flavored soda by Virginia Dare. They were also bottling Nesbitts from 1948-1964. John A. Ottoviano was the president and Thomas Ottoviano was the manager from 1938-1965. The location on the bottles changed from Graniteville, RI to Johnston, RI sometime after 1960. Graniteville is a town located in Johnston, so maybe they thought using Johnston would be more recognizable. They were bought out by the Rose Beverage Co. in 1966.

(ca. 1945-ca. 1965) ACL age (1940-1965) Beverage Co.

Batchelor's Bottling Works

George Batchelor began bottling soda in Woonsocket in 1878. His son G. Frank Batchelor took over the business in 1898. By 1911 the company had become Batchelor's Bottling Works located at the rear of 80 River Rd. Raymond Walsh was the manager from 1938-1943. Judge John J. Mee was president of the company from 1940-46. Roy B. Randall was the general manager in 1944. Raymond F. Murphy was the president from 1947-1951. George E. Keene was the manager from 1947-1948. Herbert R. Welzel was the manager from 1949-1951. Chester K. Roberts was the president from 1953-55. Antonio Lucchesi was the president from 1956-1977. Frank McDurman was the president from 1978-1981. They bottled Coca-Cola from 1927-1946. They were bottling Mission Orange soda from 1944-1945. They began to use ACL bottles in the 1940s and continued into the 1970s. In 1954 the company became Batchelor's Beverages Inc. They bottled Zimba Cola from 1947-1955. In 1956 the B.L.T.M. Bottling Co. Inc. succeeded Batchelor's Bottling Works. They continued to bottle Batchelor's Beverages and Lambert's Beverages. Batchelor's Beverages wasn't listed again until 1972-79. The B.L. & M. Bottling Co. became the L. & M. Bottling Co. in 1970. One of their last brands was Drink-Me Pop (1979-1981). Batchelor's Beverages Inc. was last listed in 1979 and became Beverage World in 1980.

(1940s-1955 Batchelors) (1956-1970 B.L. & M.) (1970-1981 L. & M.)

Bell Bottling Co.

The Bell Bottling Co. was established in Providence, RI in 1923. They were located at 73 Hope St. They were moderately successful, and by 1940 began to bottle Ritz-E brand soda. The date codes on these Glenshaw bottles can be hard to read, but I'm pretty sure they are 1940s-50s era bottles. From 1939-1959 Speros (Spiros) Karambelas and Constantine Tsagarakis were the owners. John C.

Tsagarakis and Constantine G. Tsagarakis were the owners from 1959-1962. In 1960, Berry Spring Beverages Inc., Liberty Club Inc., and Ritz-E Beverage Co. were all at this location. None of these companies were listed in 1961. Only the Bell Bottling Co. was listed in 1962. They were still in business in 1963. The Bell Bottling Co. Inc. had 7 employees in 1958. This was the only Rhode Island company to use promotional ACL saltshakers which were marked Ritz-E. They also sold Liberty Beverages for a short time. It was likely they were sued by the Supreme Mineral Water Co. who were selling Liberty Club Beverages. They were on Ives St. in 1940. They were at 115 Gano St. in 1942-46. From 1947-1962 they were at 115-117 Gano St.

(1940-1950) ACL Ritz-E (1923-1963)

Berry Spring Mineral Water Co.

The Berry Spring Mineral Water Co. dates back to 1896 but was first officially listed in 1900. During the 1920-30s, it became one of the most successful bottling companies in Rhode Island. It was at 81-89 Beverage Hill Ave. in 1935-1947. Benjamin Levin was the manager from 1927-1940. George W. Korper was the manager in 1942-1947. Mrs. Pearl R. Priest was the president from 1940-1942. The Pawtucket Beverage Co. was also at this location from 1939-1943. The Squirt Bottling Co. of RI was also at this location from 1944-1947. They bottled Orange Crush from 1944-1947. They used a small size ACL bottle in the early 1940s. In 1947 they partnered with the White Rock Bottling Co. They were bought out the next year. In 1952 the Cott Beverage Co. bought out White Rock.

(1942 ACL) (1940-1947)

Better/Beta Beverage Co.

The Better Beverage Co. of Providence produced the brand Alaska Beverages in the 1940s. The company started out as the Orange Cream Bottling Co. in 1925 and became the Beta Beverage Co. in 1936. It was at 33 Meader St. from 1936-1957. Pasquale DelVecchio was the president from 1937-1951. Donald N. Eastman and Ernest G. Johnson were the owners in 1953. Donald Eastman and John Cabral were the owners from 1954-1957. They were also bottling Golf Club Beverages from 1937-1948. They were bottling Cheer Up in 1954-1957. It was listed as Better Beverages in 1949. In 1950 it was listed as Better Beverages, also Beta Beverages. It was back to Beta in 1953. This company was listed until 1957. Some Alaska bottles say Better Beverage Co. on the back, and some say Beta. It was likely when the name first changed to Better Beverage Co., it stayed that way on the bottles.

(ca. 1940-1947) Beta (1948-1957) Better?

B. L. & M. Co.

The B.L. & M. Co. is related to Batchelor's Bottling Works and Lambert's Bottling Works. In 1954-1955 the Lambert Bottling Co. B.L.M. Inc. was listed at 80 River Rd. The B.L. & M. Bottling Co. was listed in 1956-1969 at 80 River Rd. It likely stands for Batchelor's Lucchessi & Mazzarella Co. Anthony Luccessi was the president from 1956-1971. In 1960 Antonio P. Lucchessi was the president and Cosmo T. Mazzarella was the vice president. It was also the L. & M. Bottling Co. in 1970. It became the L. & M. Bottling Co. (on ACL bottles) by 1970. They bottled Batchelor's and Lambert's Beverages from 1956-1971. Lamberts was last listed in 1976.

Cosmos T. Mozzorello was the manager in 1956. They had 14 employees. In 1957 they had 11 employees, and Antonio was listed as the manager. In 1958 it was called the B.L. & M. Bottling Works, Inc., and had 15 employees.

(1956-1970) B.L. & M. (1970-1982) L. & M.

Blue Ribbon Bottling Co.

The Blue Ribbon Bottling Co. was located in Providence. They were first listed at 69 Silver Lake Ave. in 1950 but were officially established in late 1949. The Turks Head Bottling Co. was formerly at this location. D. Thomas Testa was the owner and Thomas J. Nardolillio was the secretary in 1950-59. The Brownie Bottling Co. appears to have been bought by Blue Ribbon in 1956. They bottled Brownie Club Beverages from 1956-1966. Thomas Testa and Thomas J. Nardolillio were the owners in 1960-66. They bottled Dr. Pepper from 1962-66. They were officially bottling Brownie Club Beverages in 1966. They were not listed in 1967. By 1970 the Turks Head Beverage Co. was at this location. (Probably not, no listing in Beverage Bureau after 1966)

(1949-1966) Blue Ribbon (1956-1966) Brownie Club BR

Bridge Club Beverage Co.

The Bridge Club Beverage Co. was established in 1933. It was located at 23 Chaffee St. in Prtovidence from 1933-1940. It was at 92 Plainfield St. from 1941-1959. Bromius Simon and Alex Dialtuva were the owners from 1938-1951. Peter N. Panaretos was the owner from 1953-1959. They were using ACL bottles by 1942. They were bottling Nichol Kola from 1942-1951. They were bottling Baker's Root Beer from 1953-59. They sold out to the Eglin Sales Corp. in 1959, being unable to compete with the larger brand names.

(ca. 1942-1959)

Brooklawn

No information yet. This company I believe originated in Bridgeport, CT. One example dates to 1957.

Brownie Bottling Co.

The Colaluca Bros. established a bottling plant in Providence in 1908. In 1937 one of the founders sons, Albert Colaluca, changed the name of the company to the Brownie Bottling Co. It was at 79 Coggeshall Ave. from 1937-1946. Albert was the owner and M.A. Colaluca the manager from 1938-1943. Peter, M.A., and Albert Colaluca were the owners from 1944-47. It was at 79-93 Coggeshall St. from 1947-1951. It changed slightly to 77-93 Coggeshall St. in 1953. M.A. Colaluca was listed at the owner from 1948-1955. Albert was the manager from 1953-55. It was one of a handful of RI bottlers to have ACLs dating into the 1930s. I have confirmed this to 1939, which is close to when the company changed its name. They also bottled Grandpa's Draft Type New England Style Beverages. The company was taken over by the Blue Ribbon Bottling Co. around 1956. In 1946 they had 13 employees. They were also bottling Moxie from 1950-55. They were bottling Necco Coffee Soda from 1951-53. They were not listed in 1956.

(1937-1955)

Canada Dry Bottling Co.

The Canada Dry Bottling Co. came to Providence by 1933 but were not listed in the Beverage Bureau. From 1940-47 they also had a location at 51 S. Union St. in Pawtucket. Edwin Moran was the manager at this location. They had 14 employees in 1947. By 1945 the Ochee Spring Water Co. was bottling Spur, a brand put out by Canada Dry. They bottled Spur from 1945-1961. The vast majority of their ACL bottles have no location, but one from 1948 is marked Providence. From 1948-1961 they were bottling Hi-Spot, another Canada Dry beverage. The Canada Dry Bottling Co. was listed at 775 Hartford Ave., the location of the Ochee Spring Water Co. in 1950. They were bottling Canada Dry Ginger Ale, Sparkling Water, Spur, and Hi-Spot. From 1953-1960 they were bottling "the complete line of Canada Dry" products. They had 25 employees from 1956-57, in Johnston. Alice L. Steeves was the president from1953-1961. They had 26 employees in Providence in 1958. The Ochee Spring Water Co. was not listed in 1962.

Spur (1945-1961) Canada Dry (1945?) (1948-1961)

Clover Club Bottling Co.

The Clover Club Bottling Co. succeeded the Hebe Beverage Co. in 1943. It was at rear 10-24 Spruce St. in Providence in1944. Frank Salk was the owner. John F. Timothy and William H. Garrahan were the owners from 1945-1950. Only William was listed from 1950-54. It was at 173 Atwells Ave. from 1945-1951. They bottled Red Rock Cola from 1945-1956. In 1952-1963 they were at 387 Charles St. Miss. H. Lynd Murphy was the owner from 1955-1966. They were at 38 Oriental St. from 1964-66. They specialized in ginger ale and also bottled sparkling water. They used paper labels for their quart size bottles while they were using smaller size ACL bottles.

In 1960 Miss H. Lynd Murphy was the manager, and Mrs. Harold Congdon the secretary. They were at 387 Charles St. building 4. The company had 8 employees. They had 6 employees in 1958-59. They were not listed in 1967.

(1943-1966)

Coca-Cola Bottling Co.

The Coca-Cola Bottling Co. came to RI in the early 1900s. They first opened a plant in Providence, and shortly after in Woonsocket and Newport. The Woonsocket plant was short-lived, and in the 1943 the last plant was opened in Peace Dale. Coca-Cola took their time transitioning to ACL bottles, starting in 1957. So far the earliest examples in RI date to the mid-1960s and continue into the 1970s. The Peace Dale and Newport plants closed in the 1970s, while the Providence plant is still in operation. For two years (mainly 1968) the brand Simba was test-marketed in Rhode Island, Massachusetts, and Texas. The bottle is not marked, but some of the caps say "bottled in Providence, RI", so it is considered a RI ACL.

The Providence plant was at 95 Pleasant Valley Parkway from 1940 topresent.

The Newport plant produced Newport Club Beverages (an ACL bottle) in the 1950s. P. Faerber & Sons Co. Inc. were bottling Coca-Cola in 1950. In 1951 the Coca-Cola Bottling Co. of Newport took over P. Faerber & Sons Co. but Louis F. Faerber was still the president and manager. It was at 43 Memorial Blvd. from 1953-1977. Louis was the president from 1951-1978. The Newport plant was not listed in 1978.

They were bottling Fanta, Tab, and Sprite in 1973.

The Peace Dale plant at 43 Kersey Rd. produced South County Beverages (and ACL bottle) starting around 1950 and continuing to at least 1973. C.W. Hodgson was the president and Samuel Holden the manager from 1945-1947. Samuel was replaced by Richard Van Iderstine in 1948. Arthur S. Hassell was the president and Richard Van Iderstine was the manager in 1950. Arthur from 1951-1960. Charles B. White was the president in 1973. In 1973 the New London, CT plant was bottling the soda for this location including Fanta, Tab, Sprite, and Fresca. The plant was closed by 1974.

(1957-1970s) Providence
(1957-1973) (1968) Peace Dale (1951-1959) South County Beverages
(1957-1977) Newport

Cott Beverage Co.

The Cott Beverage Co. of New Haven, Ct. opened a bottling plant in Pawtucket, RI in 1952. They bought out the White Rock Bottling Co. of RI, which was formerly the Berry Spring Mineral Water Co. According to the Beverage Bureau, the company was owned by the Eastern Co. of Cambridge, Mass. It was at 81-89 Beverage Hill Rd. from 1952-1971. Allen Steinert was the president from 1952-1964 and John F. Kitson the manager from 1952-1955. Thomas F. Reilly was the manager in 1956-57. Arthur Hogan was the manager from 1958-1967. Joseph P. Maloney was the president from 1965-1967. John J. Cott was the president from 1968-1972. Robert H. Kitson was the manager in 1968. They had 15 employees in 1956-57, and 17 employees from 1958-1960. It became the Cott Corporation in 1970. In 1966-1971 they were bottling Cott Quality Beverages, Cott Quality Dietetic Beverages, and Metri-Cola Diet Cola. In 1972 they moved to 5 Dunnellen Rd. in East Providence. They were not listed in 1973.

(1952-1971)

Cotton Club Beverage Co.

The Cotton Club Beverage Co. came to Cranston, RI in the 1940s. They were using ACL bottles by 1945 and continued into the 1950s. The company started in Ohio, and eventually had franchises across the US. While not advertised, I believe the National Bottling Co. bottled Cotton Club soda since they were the only bottling company in Cranston in the 1940s. Sophie Cook was the owner at 6 Byron St. from 1940-1952. E.J. Dybala took over the National Bottling Co. in 1952. It became the E.J. Dybala Bottling Works in 1954. From 1953-1968 the Cotton Club Soda Co. was listed at the same location. They were at 275 Niantic Ave. from 1953-1968. Edward J. Dybala was the owner. Both companies were not listed in 1969. Hope Club Beverages moved to this location in 1972.

(1945-1951?) (1952-1968)

Deep Rock Co.

The Deep Rock Spring was located in Nayatt, RI (a village in West Barrington). It was one of the most prolific bottling companies in RI. This company was started in 1919. By the mid-1930s, Deep Rock Co. began manufacturing soda on Washington Rd., and it is likely they used water from the spring for this operation. They were one of the first companies to use ACL soda bottles in RI, with the earliest example dating to 1937. Brands they produced include Alka-Time, Deep Rock, Dr. Swett's Root Beer, King Orange Soda, and Xtra. In 1944-47 they were bottling Xtra, 7-Up, Dr. Swett's, and Tru-Ade. In 1948-1957 they were just bottling 7-Up and Tru-Ade.

They also bottled Hires Root Beer from 1958-1974, but these bottles are not marked Deep Rock. The Tru-Ade and Seven-Up bottles are marked West Barrington. They were at 385 Washington Rd. in 1954-1985. They were bottling Hires, 7-Up, and Crush in 1975-77. They stopped bottling Tru-Ade in 1975. They also bottled Dr. Pepper from 1978-1980. They were added Diet 7-Up, Royal Crown, and Diet Rite in 1981. They added RC 100 in 1983. They added Crush and Squirt in 1986.

The company had 21 employees in 1953. They had 24 employees in 1956, 26 in 1957, 25 in 1958, 32 in 1959, and 30 in 1960.

Clifford M. Wilson was the owner from 1937-1954. Deep Rock Inc. was managed by Peter Picerelli from 1945-1954. He served as president from 1955-1962. Marie Picerelli was the president from 1963-1972. Robert F. Killian was the president from 1973-1979. Ray Wasser was the president in 1980. Samuel Baker was the president and Ray Wasser the manager in 1981. Ray was the owner until 1983. Samuel Erdman was the president in 1984. In 1978 they had a warehouse at 400 Knight St.

Warwick, the former location of the Royal Crown Bottling Co. In 1984 they had 14 trucks and 33 employees. From 1976-1980 it was at 376 Washington Rd. It was at 385 Washington St. in 1980-85. In 1984 an article stated that the "Deep Rock Corp." was moving to Warwick.

In 1986 Deep Rock Inc. moved to 101 Jefferson Boulevard in Warwick. This was the location of the Jefferson Bottling Co. They were at this location until 1993.

(1937-1942 (48?)) Deep Rock

(1938) Alka-Time

(1940) Dr. Swett's Root Beer (1944-1947)

(1941) King Orange Soda

(1946-1963) Seven-Up (1944-1993)

(1942-1965) Tru-Ade (1947-1974)

(1941) Xtra (1944-1947)

Dexter Bottling Co.

The Dexter Bottling Co. was established in Central Falls in 1921. That year it was located at 20 Tiffany St. Later they moved to 194 Washington St. They used ACL bottles in the 1950s. Brands they produced include Dexter and Daly-Aid. Edmond & Eva LaPlume were the owners from 1942-1957. Leo & Lillian LaPlume were the owners from 1958-1959. Leo LaPlume was the owner in 1960-68. In 1968-1971 Lillian LaPlume was the owner. Norman G. Larivee joined the company as the manager in 1970. It was back at 185 Washington St. from 1959-1965. It was at 187 Washington St. in 1970. They were not listed in 1972.

(1955-1958?) Dexter

(1960) Daly Aid

E.J. Dybala Bottling Works

The Edward J. Dybala Bottling Works were established in 1952 in Cranston, RI. Edward left the J.M. Dybala Bottling Works in Woonsocket for the National Bottling Co. In 1954 the Cotton Club Soda Co. and National Bottling Co. were also listed at this location. They might have used ACL bottles in the 1950s, and advertised themselves as "Cranston's only soda plant." They appear to have copied the bottle styles of Dybala's Spring of Woonsocket, using nearly identical small size deco bottles and large ACL quarts. They were bottling Bireley's from 1956-1968. They were not listed in 1969. They were succeeded by the Hope Club Beverage Co. in 1972.

(1952-1968)

Dybala's Spring Bottling Works

John M. Dybala was bottling soda in Woonsocket by 1920. He formed the J.M. Dybala Bottling Works in 1926. Dybalas Spring Bottling Works was first mentioned in 1936. They might have used ACL bottles as early as 1940 and continued into the 1960s. I believe they only made quart ACLs and that the small bottles were embossed art deco. From 1948-1950 the company was known as Dybala's Spring Bottling Co. as opposed to Dybala's Bottling Works. The name changed back in 1952. They were at 46 Thomas St. from 1940-1984. They were bottling Orange Crush from 1930-1944. In 1961 Francis M. Dybala was listed as the manager. John M. Dybala was the president from 1920-1962. Francis became the president from 1963-1984. They were not listed after 1984. The company was still in business in 2000.

(1940-1984)

Eagle Bottling Co.

The Eagle Bottling Co. was established in Warren, RI in 1921. The company moved to Bristol in 1936. They were at 9 Thompson Ave. from 1936-1949. Augusto C. Ramos was the owner from 1936-1962. They were bottling Cheer Up and Pop Kola from 1950-1957. They were bottling Virginia Dare Beverages from 1959-1975. It was at 15 Bay View Ave. from 1950-1993?. In 1955 they were also at corner of Constitution & Thames St. Daniel and John P. Ramos were the owners from 1963-1975. They first used ACL bottles in the 1940s. Brands include Dub-L-Valu, Eagle, and Virginia Dare. They started to bottle Virginia Dare by 1958 and continued into the early 1970s. They were not listed in 1976.

(1940) Dub-L-Valu
(1946) Eagle
(1958-1975) Virginia Dare

Echo Spring Bottling Co.

Moren & Sullivan took over T.M. Morris & Co. in 1931. They started bottling Echo spring water around the same time. Sullivan left the partnership in 1934, and Anthony Moren created the Echo Spring Bottling Co. It was listed from 1934-1944 at 300 Thames St. In 1934-1950 Anthony A. Moren was the proprietor. Oddly in 1944-48 the Beverage Bureau said Moren & Sullivan were also at that location. From 1945-19 it was at Thames St., cor. Constitution St. (BB) It was on Constitution St. in 1940-1954. In 1946 Marguerite A. Moran joined the company as the manager. From 1949-1954 they were bottling Echo Beverages. From 1950-54 Anthony and Marguerite Moran were the owners and Richard A. Moran was the manager. The company was not listed in 1955.

(1949-1954)

Empire Beverages

The Empire Bottling Works was established in Bristol, RI in 1930. In 1930 the company was at 155 Bradford St. From 1936-1986 it was at 43 Thompson Ave. Antonio Borges was the owner from 1936-1940. Fortunada S. Borges (his wife) was the president from 1940-1950. Antonio the manager from 1940-46. Joseph R. Borges was the manager from 1947-1950. Antonio was listed as the president again from 1951-53. Joseph R. Borges was the president in 1954. Antonio was the president again from 1955-1966. Edward R. Borges was the manager from 1955-1965. Edward was the owner from 1965-19. In 1948 it was called Empire Club Beverages. They moved to 61 Buttonwood St. in 1987 and are still in business there today. They first used ACL bottles in the early 1970s and continued into the 1980s. They are still in business today.

(1974-1984)

Frisky Bottling Co.

The Frisky Botting Co. of RI was located in Providence. In 1949-1960 it was at the same location as the Lobello Spring & Soda Water Co. (aka Wellington Club Beverages from 1950-53) at 828 Charles St. Albert R. Lobello was the owner in 1949. Marguerite Lobello was the owner and Albert Lobello the manager in 1955. I have an ACL dated 1947, which I tentatively consider a RI ACL. The company had a main location in Connecticut.

(1947) (1949-1960)

Girard Spring Water Co.

The Girard Spring Water Co. was established in North Providence around 1897. They were located at 1100 Mineral Spring Ave. from 1920-1980+. W.B. Baldwin was the owner from 1940-1943. G.J. Ponton was the owner from 1944-1959. They were using ACL sodas by the late 1940s and continued into the 1960s. Armand Ponton was the owner from 1960-1982. In 1971 John B. Ponton joined the company as the vice president. V. Florence Ponton was the president from 1983-1986. John B. Ponton was the president from 1987-1993+. The company is still in business today.

(1948-1960s)

Glee Club

Barnet Weinbaum was a bottler in Providence. He started his business in the early 1900s. In 1939 he established the Weinbaum Bottling Co. It was at 132 Willard Ave. in 1939. They were bottling Glee Club Beverages from 1944-1950. It was at 10-1/2 Paca Place from 1940-1948. Anna Weinbaum was the owner from 1944-1950. It was at 29 Hilton St. from 1949-1952. It was at 27 Hilton St. from 1953-1957. In 1951 the company officially became Glee Club Beverages. John J. Alexion was the president from 1951-1953. Nathan S. Beckett the vice president/treasurer from 1951-1953. Nathan was the president from 1954-1969. The company moved to 80 Rock Ave. in Warwick in 1958-59. It was at 70 Rock Ave. from 1960-69. They were not listed in 1970. They used ACL bottles in the 1940s.

(1941-1947)

Havens Bottling Works

The Havens Bottling Works was established in the 1922 by Charles D. Havens in Westerly, RI. Their plant was at 5 Industrial Ave. and their office was at 58 Canal St. in 1939. They were bottling Coca-Cola from 1927-1939. They were bottling Orange Crush from 1936-1943. They were bottling Pop Kola from 1940-1950. George and Alfred Havens were the owners from 1939-1940. Jennie R. Havens and C. Alfred Havens were the owners from 1942-1950. They began to bottle Westerly Club brand soda around 1940. They went out of business in 1950. The ACLs date from 1941-1947.

(1941-1947)

Hebe Co.

The Caproni Bros. established a bottling company in Providence in the 1880s. Around 1916, they became the Hebe Co. They achieved moderate success in the 1920-30s. They were at 177 Atwells Ave. from 1939-1941. It was at rear 10-24 Spruce St. in 1943. John DeCesare was the owner from 1939-1943. Anthony DeCesare was the manager from 1942-1943. It was succeeded by Clover Club Bottling Co. in 1944.

(1940-1943)

Hope Club

The Puritan Beverage Co. was established in Providence, RI in 1938. It succeeded the Quaker Club Co. and McLaughlin's Bottling Works. It was at 47 Burnside St. Julius Moskol was the president. The company became Hope Club Beverages in 1941. Hugh Gasbarro, Anthony Tarro, and Walter Giannetti were the owners. Walter Giannetti was the president in 1942. It was at 3 Murphy St. from 1942-47. Anguileno D'Iorio was the president from 1943-47. Walter Giannetti was the treasurer and manager from 1943-1948. Walter F. Giannetti was the owner from 1949-55. Rocco Mendillo was the manager from 1951-55. It was at 3 Murphy St. or 71 Spruce St from 1948-49. It was at

71 Spruce St. from 1950-1971. They bottled Min-R-Ize from 1950-1964. They first used ACL bottles in the early 1940s and continued into the 1970s. They were very successful, and the plant moved to Cranston, RI around 1969 (definitely by 1972). Anthony George was the owner in 1956-1986. Gary George was the owner from 1987-1991. It was at 275 Niantic Ave. from 1972-1991. In 1984 they had two trucks and 3 employees.

(1943-1969) Providence (1968-1990) Cranston

Ideal Beverage Co.

The Ideal Beverage Co. was located in Central Falls, RI. It succeeded the Riverside Beverage Co. It was initially at 8 Hartford Ave. in Riverside from 1941-44. Albert Laliberte was the owner, and Lucien Laliberte the manager from 1941-1954. It was at 20 Tiffany St. Central Falls from 1945-48. It was at 57 Earle St., Central Falls from 1944 (1949)-1960. Albert & Lucien Laliberte were the owners. They were also bottling Wildfire from 1949-50. Normand W. Bilodeau was the president from 1955-1957. Normand Bilodeau and Albert Laliberte were the owners from 1958-59. It was back to just Normand in 1960. They used ACL bottles in the 1940s, and probably went out of business in late 1960.

(1941-1947 ACL) (1951-1960)

Kerona Co.

James Keron established a bottling company in Central Falls in the 1880s. He bottled a drink called Herbola. The company later became known as the Central Falls Bottling Co. The Kerona Co. was first listed in 1931 as part of the Central Falls Bottling Co. Frank Keron was the owner at this time. It was at 15 North St. from 1915-1970+. In 1933 Mary F. Keron became the administrator. In 1936 the name officially changed to The Kerona Co. They used water from the Deep Rock Spring. Thomas L. Kerona was the president from 1936-1947. Francis L. Kerona was the president from 1948-1961. They bottled Mission Orange from 1942-1948. William A. Murphy Jr. was the president from 1962-1970. The company used quart ACL bottles in the mid-late 1940s. It appears the company then capitalized on their Old English brand soda, which it made an ACL bottle for as late as 1963. The plain Kerona bottles were made as ACL quarts and embossed deco 8-ounce bottles while Old English was sold in ACL 7-ounce bottles and paper labeled quarts. The company went out of business by late 1970.

(ca. 1940-1970)
(1944-1948) Kerona
(1963) Old English

L. & M. Bottling Co.

The L. & M. Bottling Co. was formerly the B.L. & M. Bottling Co. Antonio P. Lucchessi was the president and Cosmo T. Mazzarella the vice president. It was first listed in 1954 as the successor to the Lambert Bottling Co. It was at 590 Clinton St. In 1956 it became the B.L. & M. Bottling Co. The name changed back to L. & M. in 1970. It was at 80 River Rd. from 1970-1982. In 1971 it was still listed under B.L. & M. Bottling Co., Batchelors, Lamberts, and L.& M. Bottling Co. Michael W. Sokoll was the manager in 1977. Frank McDurman was the owner from 1978-1981. They bottled Batchelors Beverages and Drink Me Pop (1979-1981).

(1954-1955) (1970-1981)

Lambert Bottling Co.

In 1940, the Lambert Soda Works became the Lambert Bottling Co. Ludger & Olivia Lambert along with Mrs. Belhumeur were the owners from 1940-1946. Olivia Lambert and Esmeralda Belhumeur were the owners from 1947-1948. Olivia Lambert was the owner from 1949-1953. They were at 590 Clinton St. from 1940-1953. In 1954 the company became the L. & M. Bottling Co. It became the B.L. & M. Bottling Co. in 1956.

(1940-1953) Lambert (1954-1971) BLM

Liberty Club Beverages

Liberty Club Beverages was produced by the Supreme Mineral Water Co. It was first listed in 1936. It was also known as Liberty Club Beverages. It was at 8-14 W. River St. from 1936-38. Samuel LaBush was the manager from 1936-1941. George LaBush was the president from 1937-1941. Samuel was the owner and manager from 1942-1943. Samuel LaBush and Benjamin Cohen were the owners from 1944-1954. Benjamin Cohen died in 1954. Martin Mondlick was the receiver in 1956. It was at 69 Bath St. from 1939-1956. Their earliest ACL dates to 1942. In 1948 the drink Lime-Up was produced by "Liberty Club Beverages". They were not listed in 1957.

(1942-1956) Liberty
(1948) Lime-Up

Liberty Club Soda Water Co.

The Liberty Club Soda Water Co. might be related to the Supreme Mineral Water Co. They bottled Yankee brand beverages. They used ACL bottles dating from 1941 to the 1950s.

(1941-1953)

Lobello Spring and Soda Water Co.

The Lobello Spring and Soda Water Co. was established in the 1926 in Providence, RI. It was at 828 Charles St. from 1927-1960. Antonio Lobello was the owner from 1926-1955 Peter J. Lobello joined the company as the manager from 1948-51. Albert A. Lobello was the manager from 1953-1960. Margherita Lobello was the owner from 1956-1960. Albert Lobello was the president and manager from 1961-1963. They bottled Frisky in 1949. They began to bottle Wellington Club brand soda in the mid-1940s. In 1950 the company became Wellington Club Beverages and was also home to the Frisky Bottling Co. of RI. In 1956 it became the Lobello Spring Water & Soda Co. again. They were bottling Frisky, D-Lish, and Wellington Club Beverages from 1956-1963. They were not listed in 1964. Recently a bottle called Tweed Beverages was discovered that was also bottled by this company in 1944.

(1940s-1964)

Ma's Old Fashioned Root Beer Bottling Co.

In 1954 Ma's partnered with Mission Orange Bottling Co. at 63 Arnold St. The partnership lasted until 1969.

(1954-1969)

Mission/ M. & M. Bottling Co.

The Mission Orange Bottling Co. moved to 484 Manville Rd. in 1956. The name changed to the Mission Bottling Co. in 1959. That year they were bottling Ma's Old Fashioned Root Beer and Quiky. Albert DaCosta and Armond Berard were the owners. In 1970 they also began to bottle Manhattan

Beverages, while discontinuing Ma's Root Beer. The company became the Mission & Manhattan Bottling Works, Inc. in 1972. Carolyn Chapdelaine was the president and Albert J. DaCosta the manger. In 1978 Inacio Tributino became the president, treasurer, and manager. They were bottling Mission Orange, Manhattan, and Quicky at the time. The company was not listed from 1980-81. It was back in 1982. From 1985-87 it was listed as the Mission Bottling Works. It was located at 484 Manville Rd. from 1972-1987. It was not listed in 1988.

(1972-1987)

Manhattan Bottling Co.

The Esmond Spring Soda Works was established in Esmond, RI in 1929. By the 1940s they were bottling Manhattan Club brand soda. Homer Sweeney was the owner. It became the Manhattan Bottling Co. Inc. in 1945. In was at 55 Esmond St. from 1945-1949 and 1953-1958. John Iannotti was the president from 1945-1949 and 1953-1958. Vito J. DelDeo was the manager from 1945-1949 and 1953-1958. They first used ACL bottles in the early 1940s. The earliest ACL bottle is marked Esmond, RI. In 1950 the company moved to in Cranston, and was being bottled by the National Bottling Co. Michael A. Iannotti was the president. They were at 8 Byron St. They were not listed in 1951-52. In 1953-58 they were back in Esmond. They were not listed again from 1959-1970. In 1971 Manhattan Beverages were being bottled by the Mission Bottling Co. of Woonsocket. They used ACL bottles in the 1970s. The newest ACL bottle was bottled by the L. & M. Bottling Co.

(1940-1949) Esmond (1950-1958) of RI (1970-1987) Woonsocket

Martins Soda Works

Martins Soda Works was established in Woonsocket in the 1931. It succeeded the short-lived Eureka Bottling Works. Horace Martin was the owner from 1931-1947. It was at 434 Rathbun St. from 1931-1946. They bottled Orange Kist from 1940-46. Roland G. Sicard was the owner from 1948-1964. Alva P. Rondeau was the owner from 1965-1968. No owner was listed in 1969. It was at 444 Rathbun St. from 1947-49. They bottled Frostie Old-Fashioned Root Beer from 1949-1951. It was at rear 444 Rathbun St. from 1950-1968. In 1952-57 they bottle Squirt. They bottled Virginia Dare from 1963-1969. It became Martins Soda Works, Inc. in 1961. It was not listed in 1970. An ACL bottle dating to 1949 has been reported.

(ca. 1940-1969)

Mission Orange Bottling Co.

The Mission Orange Bottling Co. originated from California. It was officially listed in Woonsocket in 1948, but it was first opened in 1946. It was formerly the Tip-Top Beverage Co., which was oddly not listed in any directory. They were located at 63 Arnold St. from 1946-1955. Alfred Fregesu and Albert DaCosta were the owners from 1946-1951. Albert J. DaCosta and Armond Berard were the owners from 1953-1968. Albert DaCosta was the owner from 1969-19. They were located at 484 Manville Rd. from 1956-1973. They were also bottling Ma's Old-Fashioned Root Beer from 1954-1969. They bottled Quicky from 1959-1971. Albert J. DaCosta was the owner. In 1959 the name changed to Mission Bottling Co. They bottled Manhattan Beverages in 1970. In 1972 it became the M. & M. Bottling Co. (Mission and Manhattan). In was listed in 1973 as bottling Manhattan Beverages. Albert was still the owner.

(1946-1972) (1957-1967 ACL)

Location: Likely intact, building set back from the road

Moose Head Beverage Co.

The Moose Head Beverage Co. was established in Providence in 1936. It succeeded Turbitt & Co. It was at 119 Gano St. from 1936-1940. It was at 30 Sheldon St. from 1941-1950. Larry Gomes was the president in 1936. Mary Gomes was the president from 1937-1943. Anthony H. Gomes was the manager from 1939-1943. Ralph A. York was the owner from 1944-1947. They were using ACL bottles by the early 1940s. They bottled 7-Up from 1944-46. They bottled Yankee Doodle Root Beer from 1946-47. In 1948-1950 they were also bottling 7-Up for their Attleboro, Mass. plant. M.T. And Ralph A. York were the owners from 1948-1950. M.J. Brown was the manager from 1949-1950. They were not listed in 1951.

(ca. 1940-1950)

Ochee Spring Water Co.

The Ochee Spring Water Co. was established in the early 1900s. Water from the spring had been bottled since 1886. The spring and bottling plant were located in Johnston, but they had an office in Providence. From 1920-1940 they were located at 745 Hartford Ave. They were at 775 Hartford Ave. from 1941-1961. Arthur P. Angell was the owner from 1935-1939. Harry L. Steeves was the manager from 1940-1950. Mrs. Alice L. Steeves was the owner from 1951-1961. By 1940 the company used ACL bottles. They bottled Spur from 1945-1961. They bottled Hi-Spot from 1948-1961. In 1950 the Canada Dry Bottling Co. of RI partnered with them. That year they bottled Canada Dry Ginger Ale, Canada Dry Sparkling Water, Hi-Spot, and Spur. Arthur J. Boucher was the plant manager from 1955-1961. They bottled Canada Dry Spur, Ledge Brand and Ochee Club Soda and Ginger Ale. They were last listed in 1961.

(ca. 1940-1961)

Pepsi-Cola

Pepsi-Cola was not bottled in RI until 1940 when Pepsi joined with the Warwick Club Ginger Ale Co. Before this, Warwick Club had a partnership with their rival Coca-Cola. For a few tense years (1940-43), Pepsi-Cola and Coca-Cola were bottled side by side before Warwick Club severed ties with Coke completely in 1944. This facility was located at 108 Pond St. and is still standing today. Marked ACLs date from the mid-1940s to the mid 1950s. The first RI Pepsi bottles had paper labels in the early 1940s. The last marked RI Pepsi dates to around 1958-1960, when the design changed to the swirl bottle. In 1971 Pepsi bought out Warwick Club Beverages. Frank Baker was the president in 1973. They were also bottling Schweppes at that time. Pepsi was not listed in RI from 1974-1980 but was back at 1400 Pontiac Ave. Cranston in 1981. Pepsi is still bottled in RI on Pontiac Ave. in Cranston.

(ca. 1940-ca. 1960 ACL)

Red Fox Ginger Ale Co.

The Red Fox Ginger Ale Co. was established in Providence, RI in 1939. It was originally a brand created by the U.S. Bottling Co. circa 1923. It quickly achieved success and became one of the largest bottling companies in RI. It was located at 142 Livingston St. from 1939-1946. Samuel Gerstein and Abraham Goldberg were the owners from 1939-1957. Samuel M. Gerstein was the owner from 1958-1980. Harold L. Gerstein was the owner from 1981-1984. David Potter was the owner from 1985-1987. Julian Angelone was the president from 1988-1990. They bottled Empire Beverages from 1942-1955. They bottled X-Tra in 1948-1955. They bottled Nugget Beverages from 1956-1964, although the bottles date as early as 1944. They bottled Squirt from 1958-1967. They bottled No-Cal from 1965-1987. They were at 77 Silver Spring St. from 1948-1990. The company had 19 employees in 1947. It had 25 employees from 1956-1960. From 1961-1970, the Nugget Beverages Co. was also at this location. In 1984 David Potter became the new owner and a news article said he expected a good year for the company. The company was now known as Red Fox Inc. They were using ACL bottles by 1944 for their Nugget brand soda, as well as Spike-It. They didn't use an ACL for their Red Fox brand until 1951. They used ACLs into the 1970s before going out of business in 1991.

(ca. 1944-1970s)

Word Mark SPIKE-IT (CANCELLED) : Extracts, Syrups, and Concentrates Used in Making Soft Drink Beverages, and Nonalcoholic Soft Drink Beverages. FIRST USE: 1940. FIRST USE IN COMMERCE: 1940 Filing Date March 7, 1941 Registration Date July 8, 1941 Owner (REGISTRANT) Green & Green Firm composed of J. B. Green, R. H. Green, and A. M. Green (United States citizens) CORPORATION UNITED STATES 2000 Providence Street Houston TEXAS (LAST LISTED OWNER) Green & Green, Inc. Indianapolis INDIANA

Red Rock Co.

The Red Rock Bottling Co. had a franchise with the Clover Club Beverage Co. in Providence, RI. It was first listed in 1945 at 173 Atwells Ave. John F. Timothy and William H. Garrahan were the owners. It was last listed in 1956.

(1945-1956)

Riverside Beverages

Riverside Beverage Inc. was located in Riverside, RI. Milton M. Fuld was the treasurer in 1939. It was at 185 E. Knowlton St. from 1939-1940. Aldric Cloutier was the president in 1940.

By 1942 it had become the Ideal Beverage Co., located at 8 Hartford Ave. (right off of E. Knowlton St.).

(1939-1941?)

Rose Beverage Co.

The Rose Beverage Co. was established in 1910 in Providence. Originally it was the Rose Spring Water Co., which was listed from 1930-1948. The Rose Beverage Co. was officially established in 1948. It was first listed in at 10 Lynde St. from 1949-1965. Samuel A. Place was the owner from 1949-1960. George E. Freeman was the manager from 1958-1960. He was the owner from 1961-1974. By 1950 they were using ACL bottles. They bought out the Bare Rock Spring Bottling Co. in Johnston in 1966 and moved their business to the new location. They were at 250 Putnam Ave. from 1966-1974. They continued to use ACL bottles into the early 1970s. In 1975 they were bought by the RI Fruit Syrup Co. They also bottled Virginia Dare brand soda from 1966-1974.

(1948-1965) Providence (1966-1974) Johnston

Royal Crown Bottling Co.

The Royal Crown Bottling Co. came to Providence, RI in the 1940s. The Shiloh Bottling Co. formed a franchise with Royal Crown in 1943. They were at 116 Lester St. from 1943-1965 They bottled Nehi and Royal Crown brand soda. The Nehi ACLs date to the early 1950s, and the Royal Crown ACLs to the mid-1940s. In 1949 the Shiloh Bottling Co. moved while the Royal Crown Bottling Co. of RI stayed at the Lester St. address. J Milton Swartz was the president from 1949-1965. Einar F. Nerness was the general manager from 1950-1957. Later style Royal Crown bottles (from the 1950s-60s) were not marked with a location. They had 30 employees in 1956. There were 25 employees in 1957. Raymond Wasser was the manager from 1958-1965. He was also the president from 1966-1977. They had 35 employees from 1958-1960. They bottled Diet Rite and Nehi from 1966-1977. They bottled Dr. Pepper from 1972-1977. In 1973 they were listed as a subsidiary of the Cambridge Beverage Corp. in Massachusetts. They were at 101 Jefferson Blvd. Warwick from 1966-1973. They were at 400 Knight St. from 1974-1977. One directory has a location of 49 Parker St. Woonsocket in 1967. This might have been a warehouse. They were not listed in 1978.

(1943-ca. 1960 ACL) (1943-1978)

Seven-Up

The Seven-Up Bottling Co. came to RI in the 1940s. In 1942 they had a bottling plant at 15 Oak St. in North Providence. They formed partnerships with Deep Rock in West Barrington and Surf Club in Middletown. From 1944-1946, the 7-Up Newport Bottling Co. was located at the Surf Club Ginger Ale Co. on Purgatory Rd. George H. Cottle was the owner. In 1947, 7-Up bought out Surf Club Beverages. They claimed to have been established since 1937. They were at Second Beach Ave. from 1947-1950. Gladys B. and George H. Cottle were the owners from 1947-1948. George was the owner again in 1949. Beverly A. Bogert was the president and William T. King the manager in 1950. In 1949 it became the 7-Up Bottling Co. of Southern RI. They only used ACL bottles, and the RI ones date from the mid-1940s-1950. It was not listed in 1951.

The Deep Rock partnership started in 1944 and lasted until 1993.

(1944-1948) 7-Up Newport
(1949-1950) Middletown
(1944-1993) West Barrington

Shiloh Bottling Co.

The Shiloh Bottling Works was established in Providence in 1920. In 1920 the company was located at 427 Chalkstone Ave. They were at 116 Lester St. from 1935-1948. They were at 350 Dexter St. from 1949-1954. Benjamin Robin was the president from 1935-1945. Samuel Lozow was the manager from 1935-1945. Benjamin Robin and Sydney Kaplan were the owners in 1946. Sydney Kaplan was the owner from 1947-1948. Edward Duffy was the manager in 1947. Benjamin Robin was the manager in 1948. He was the owner again from 1949-1954. In 1929 the company became the Shiloh Bottling Co. They partnered with the Royal Crown Bottling Co. from 1943-1949. They first used ACL sodas in the 1940s. They were bottling Orange Crush in 1935, then again from 1949-1954. They were last listed in Providence in 1954. In 1955 the company moved to 165 Front St. in Pawtucket and was renamed the Schultz Beverage Co. Inc. Frank P. Queen was the owner. In 1956 the name was changed back to Shiloh Beverage Co. They were not listed in 1957.

(ca. 1940-1954)

Squirt Bottling Co.

The Squirt Bottling Co. opened a plant in Providence in the 1960s. They were first listed in Pawtucket at 4 Charlton Ave. in 1943. This was the location of the Berry Spring Mineral Water Co. The Squirt Bottling Co. of RI was first listed under Berry Spring in 1944. The White Rock Bottling Co. of RI succeeded the Berry Spring Mineral Water Co. in 1947 but continued to bottle Squirt until 1950. They were at 81-89 Beverage Hill Ave. from 1948-1950. Red Fox Beverages bottled Squirt from 1958-1967. The only dated ACL bottle I have is from 1964.

(1944-1950) Squirt of RI
(1958-1967) Providence

Star Bottling Co.

The Star Bottling Co. was established in Pawtucket in 1921. In 1922 they were at 7 Woodbine St. They were located at 307 Fountain St. in Pawtucket from 1922-1961. Highk Krikorian was the owner from 1930-1947. Mrs. Annie Krikorian was the treasurer in 1948. She was also the president from 1949-1958. Leo Krikorian was the manager from 1949-1958. Leo was the owner from 1959-1961. They first used ACL bottles around 1940. They were last listed in 1961.

(ca. 1940-1950s ACL) (1921-1961)

Supreme Mineral Water Co.

The Supreme Mineral Water Co. was established in Providence probably in 1936. They produced Liberty Club brand soda. They used ACL bottles from the early 1940s-1950s. In 1956 Martin Mondlick was the receiver. They were located at 69 Bath St. They were not listed in 1957.

(1936-1956) See Liberty Club

Town Club Beverage Co.

The Town Club Beverage Co. was located in Middletown, RI. It succeeded the Tobak Beverage Co. From 1943-45 the Tobak Beverage Co. bottled Town Club Beverages. It might have been bottling them since 1940. It was located at 7 Carroll Ave. from 1940-45. William Newman, Ernest Fineman, and Annie F. Harriet were the owners from 1942-45. The company moved from Newport to Middletown in 1946. It was on Aquidneck Ave. from 1946-1952. William D. Newman was the owner from 1946-1957. It was located at 613 Aquidneck Ave. from 1953-57. The ACL bottles from this plant date from the mid-late 1940s. They were not listed in 1958.

(1943-1957)

Tru-Ade Bottling Co.

The Tru-Ade Bottling Co. partnered with Deep Rock in West Barrington, RI in the 1940s. They used ACL bottles from the early 1940s to the 1960s. It was last bottled in 1974.

(ca. 1940-1960s) (-1974)

TRU ADE NOT CARBONATED Non-Alcoholic, Maltless Beverage Used as a Soft Drink and Concentrates and Extracts for Preparing the Same. FIRST USE: 1938. FIRST USE IN COMMERCE: 1938 Filing Date September 22, 1942

Twin City Spring Beverage Co.

The Twin City Spring Beverage Co. was established in Central Falls, RI in 1927. It was called the Twin City Bottling Co. from 1936-1939. It became the Twin City Beverage Co. in 1940. It became the Twin City Spring Soda Works (or Beverage Co.) in 1949. They first used ACL bottles circa 1949. They were at 9 Notre Dame St. from 1929-1935 and 1940-1963. The compsny was at 92 Hadwin St. from 1936-39. Barbara Chrupcala was the owner from 1939-1963. Thaddeus W. Chrupcala was the manager from 1949-1963. They were not listed in 1964.

(1949-1963) Beverage Co. era

Virginia Dare

See Bare Rock Beverage Co., Eagle Beverages, and Rose Beverage Co.

United Bottling Works

The United Bottling Works was located in Bristol, RI. It was established in 1947. They located at 248 Wood St. from 1948-1962 and 1966-1977. Edward S. Proto, Nicholas L. Proto, and Andrew P. DelToro were the owners in 1948. The company became Seacrest Beverages (also United Bottling Works) in 1949. It went back to United Bottling Works (bottling Seacrest Beverages) in 1951. They produced Seacrest brand Beverages, which came in an ACL bottle. The one known example dates to 1948. Edward S. Proto, Nicholas L. Proto, Gaetano Proto and Andrew P. DelToro were the owners from 1949-1953. Domenico Proto was the manager from 1949-1953. He was also the owner and manager from 1954-1962. They were not listed from 1963-1965. They were back in 1966. Guy & Edward Proto were the owners from 1966-1977. They were not listed in 1978.

(1947-1962) (1966-1977)

Warwick Club Ginger Ale Co.

The Warwick Bottling Works were established in West Warwick circa 1902. In 1930 the name changed to the Warwick Club Ginger Ale Co. They were located at 108 Pond St. from 1930-1970. Fred Clarke (1875-1952?) was the owner from 1935-1954. Luke Clarke (1902-1987) was the manager from 1951-1954. He was also the owner from 1955-1970. They bottled Fudgy from 1953-1957. They bottled Schweppes from 1956-1970. They bottled Moxie from 1957-1972. They first used ACL bottles in the late 1940s. They also bottled Speedball, an orange soda, starting in the early 1950s and continuing into the 1960s. In 1940 they partnered with Pepsi-Cola and shared the same building. They made ACLs into the 1970s. The Warwick Club Ginger Ale Co. was last listed in 1970. In 1971 Pepsi bought out Warwick Club. They continued to bottle Warwick Beverages from 1971-72. They were not listed in 1973. Pepsi in 1946, not in 1956

(ca. 1948-ca. 1972 ACL)

Yacht Club

Harry Sharp (d. 1975) came to the US in the early 1900s. For a while he bottled soda under his own name. In 1915 he opened the Yacht Club Bottling Works. It was located at 2253 Mineral Spring Ave. in Centerdale. The company became moderately successful and is one of a handful that is still in business in RI. ACL sodas date from about 1940 to the 1970s. There might be a 1930s ACL, as one was reported. They bottled Pop-Kola from 1944-1951. In 1949-1950 they were also bottling Cherry Blossoms. They bottled Frostie Root Beer from 1953-1958. They bottled Orange Crush from 1953-1958. Arthur M. Sharp (d. 1996) was the manager from 1933-1939. He was also the owner from 1940-1962. In 1963 John Sgambato became the owner. The quart sized ACL bottles are still used today, while the smaller size now has a paper label.

(ca. 1940-1970s ACL)

RI ACL Sodas List

Brand name, location
Alpha-numeric designation
Bottle color, size, label colors
Label key theme, noted if deco
Slogan (if it has one)
Bottling company name
Bottle manufacturer
Date from date code

Alaska Beverages—Providence, RI (scarce)

AK-1
Clear and green, 32oz., white and red ACL
Mountain in background, art deco neck
Better Beverage Co.
The Peak of Perfection
Contents One Full Quart embossed on heel
Reed Glass Co.
1948

AK-2
Clear, 32oz., white and red ACL
Mountain in background, art deco neck, red outline
Beta Beverage Co.
The Peak of Perfection
Contents One Full Quart embossed on heel
Reed Glass Co.
1947

AK-3
Clear, quart, white and red ACL
Mountain in background, art deco neck, no red outline
Beta Beverage Co.
The Peak of Perfection
Contents One Full Quart embossed on heel
Reed Glass Co.
1940

AK-4
Clear, 8oz., white and blue ACL (rare)
vertical ribs on shoulder
Beta Beverage Co.
Reed Glass Co.
1945, 47

Alka-Time—W. Barrington, RI (rare)

AT-1
Green, 7oz., yellow ACL
Deep Rock
Alkalize with Alka-Time, pick up and blender. Alka-Time is refreshing anytime
Numbers around front, plain bottle
Owens Illinois Glass Co.
1938

AT-2
Green, 6-1/2oz., yellow ACL
Deep Rock
Alkalize with Alka-Time, pick up and blender. Alka-Time is refreshing anytime
Numbers around front, plain bottle
Owens Illinois Glass Co.
1938

AT-3
Green, 7oz., yellow ACL
Drink it often, shoulder label
Numbers around front, plain bottle
Owens Illinois Glass Co.
1938

Batchelor's Beverages—Woonsocket, RI (12 w. colors) (most are common)

BA-1
Green, 7oz., red and white ACL (scarce)
Shield shaped front label, shield crest on shoulder
Glenshaw Glass Co.
1965

BA-2
Clear, 8oz., red and white ACL
Shield shaped front label, plain shoulder, embossed on heel and base
Bulging shoulders and heel
Batchelor's Bottling Works Inc.
Reed Glass Co.
1947

BA-3
Clear, 8oz., red and white ACL
Shield shaped front label, Batchelor's on shoulder (2x), embossed on heel and base
Bulging shoulders and heel
L. & M. Bottling Co.
Glenshaw Glass Co.
1967

BA-4
Clear, 8oz., red and white ACL
Shield shaped front label, Batchelor's on shoulder (2x), embossed on heel and base
Bulging shoulders and heel
B. L. & M. Bottling Co.
Glenshaw Glass Co.
1960, 1964

BA-5
Clear, 8oz., red and white ACL
Shield shaped front label,
Batchelor's on shoulder (2x)
L. & M. Bottling Co. Inc.
Glenshaw Glass Co.
1969, 1971

BA-6
Clear 8oz., red and white ACL
Shield shaped front label,
Batchelor's Return for
Deposit on shoulder (2x)
Plain bottle
L. & M. Bottling Co. Inc.
Glenshaw Glass Co.
1972

BA-7
Clear, 12oz., red and white ACL
Shield shaped front label,
Batchelor's Beverages on shoulder
Plain bottle, Batchelor's Bottling Works Inc.
Reed Glass Co.
1941

BA-8a
Clear, 12oz., red and white ACL
Shield shaped front label,
Batchelor's on shoulder
Stippled bottle, Batchelor's Bottling Works Inc.
Glenshaw Glass Co.
1960 (odd, should be BL&M)

BA-8b
Clear, green, 1pt. 14oz., red and white ACL
Shield shaped front label,
Batchelor's Beverages on shoulder (red outline)
Bulging shoulders and heel,
Batchelor's Bott. Wks. on base
Reed Glass Co.
1947

BA-9
Green, 1pt. 14oz., red and white ACL
Shield shaped front label,
Batchelor's Beverages on shoulder (only white)
Bulging shoulders and heel,
Batchelor's Bott. Wks. on base
Reed Glass Co.
1945?

BA-10
Clear, 1pt. 14oz., red and white ACL
Shield shaped front label,
Batchelor's Beverages on shoulder
Red shoulder label
Bulging shoulders and heel,
Batchelor's Bott. Wks. On base
Reed Glass Co.
1946

BA-11
Clear, 1pt. 14oz., red and white ACL
Shield shaped front label,
Batchelor's Beverages on shoulder
Bulging shoulders and heel,
Batchelor's Bott. Wks. on base
B. L. & M. Bottling Co.

BA-12
Clear and green, 1pt. 14oz., red and white ACL
Bottled by L. & M. Bottling Company Inc.
Shield shaped front label,
Batchelor's Beverages on shoulder
Glenshaw Glass Co.
1969

BA-13
Clear, 1pt. 14oz., red and white ACL
Return for deposit on shoulder
Shield shaped front label,
Batchelor's Beverages on shoulder
L. & M. Bottling Co. Inc.
Glenshaw Glass Co.
1972?

Batchelor's Club Soda—Woonsocket, RI (scarce)

BA-14
Clear, 7oz., white and blue ACL
Four square shield on front label, shoulder label
B.L. & M. Bottling Co. Inc.
Glenshaw Glass Co.
1963?

BA-15
Clear, 1pt. 14 fl. Oz., red and white ACL (scarce)
Rectangular label
L & M Bottling Co, Inc.
Glenshaw Glass Co.
1967

BA-16
Clear, 1pt. 14 fl. Oz., red and white ACL (scarce)
Old style rectangular label, earliest Batchelors?
? mixer and blender
Batchelor's Bottling Works, Inc.

Batchelor's Sparkling Water—Woonsocket, RI (rare)

BA-17
Clear, 7oz., red and white ACL
Shield on front
Batchelor's Beverages, Inc.
Anchor Hocking Glass Co.
1953

Berry Spring Beverages—Pawtucket, R.I. (very rare)

BE-1
Clear, 8oz., white and red ACL
Cross with rays on front
Sharpens the Appetite, Stimulates the digestion
Berry Spring Mineral Water Co. Ltd.
Owens Illinois Glass Co.
1942

BE-2
Need more info, reported 3-color ACL

Blue Ribbon Beverages—Providence, RI (rare)

BL-1
Clear, 7oz., white and blue label
Blue ribbon on front
Oil City Glass Co.
1950-52

BL-2
Clear, 28oz., white and blue label
Blue Ribbon on front
1950 (Weide)

Bridge Club Beverages—Providence, RI (13 w. colors)

BR-1
Green, 7oz., red and white ACL (rare)
Four aces on front, plain body
Hard to Beat motto
Bridge Club Bev. Co.
1955 ?

BR-2
Clear, 7oz., red and white ACL (scarce)
Four aces on front, stippled body
Hard to Beat motto
Bridge Club Bev. Co.
1951

BR-3
Clear, 8oz., red and white ACL
Four aces on front, spade and heart ACL on neck
Art deco design (rectangles with leaf vein texture on shoulder and heel)
Bridge Club Bev. Co.
Thatcher Glass Co.
1954, 55

BR-4
Clear, 9-1/4", 8oz., red and white ACL (Scarce)
Four aces on front
Art deco design (stippled rectangles on shoulder and heel)
Hard to Beat motto
Bridge Club Bev. Co.
Glenshaw Glass Co.
1947, 1951

BR-5
Clear, 8oz., red and white ACL (scarce)
Four aces on front
Art deco design (stippled rectangles on shoulder and heel)
Bridge Club Bev. Co.
Glenshaw Glass Co.
1950

BR-6
Clear, 12oz., red and white ACL (scarce-rare)
Four aces on front, slanted front label
Plain bottle
Bridge Club Bev. Co.
Glenshaw Glass Co.
N on neck- 1942

BR-7
Green, quart, red and white ACL
Four aces on front, shoulder label, Hard to Beat motto
Serve cold in clear, one full quart on back shoulder
No better beverage at any price (plain letters)
Bridge Club Bev. Co.
Glenshaw Glass Co.

BR-8
Clear and green, quart, red and white ACL (same as above)
Four aces on front, Hard to Beat motto
Serve cold in clear, one full quart on back shoulder, Telephone Elmhurst 1-8820
No Better Beverages at any price (in script)
Bridge Club Bev. Co.
Thatcher Glass Co.
1952

BR-9
Green, quart, red and white ACL
Four aces on front, Hard to Beat motto
Serve cold in red, one full quart on back shoulder
Bridge Club Bev. Co.

BR-10
Clear, green, quart, red and white ACL
Four aces on front, Bridge Club Beverages on shoulder
Clear hollow shoulder ACL
Bridge Club Bev. Co.
Glenshaw Glass Co.
Q? on lip- 1945

BR-11
Clear and green, quart, red and white ACL
Four aces on front, Bridge Club Beverages on shoulder
Solid shoulder ACL
Bridge Club Bev. Co.
Glenshaw Glass Co.
1943 or 45, 1950

Brooklawn—RI (rare)
BK-1
Clear, 7oz., red and white ACL
1947
-need picture to confirm, a Brooklawn Club exists from Bridgeport, Ct.

Brownie Club Beverages, Providence, RI (16 w. colors) (all common, green semi-common)
BC-1
Green, 7oz., red and white ACL
Elf on left, Brownie Bottling Co.
Brownie in script, plain bottle
Glenshaw Glass Co.
195?

BC-2
Clear, Green, 7oz., red and white ACL
Elf on left, Blue Ribbon Bottling Co., Inc.
Brownie in script, plain bottle (clear is stippled)
Glenshaw Glass Co.
1960 green, 1961 clear

BC-3
Clear, green, 8 oz., red and white ACL
Elf on front center, Brownie Bottling Co.
Brownie Club in block letters, not script
Art deco, stippled rectangles
Glenshaw Glass Co.
R on lip, 1946, 1947 (clear), O 1943 (green)

BC-4
Clear, 8 oz., red and white ACL
Elf on front center, Blue Ribbon Bottling Co.
Brownie is in block letters, not script
Art deco, diamond pattern
Thatcher Glass Co.
1956, 1959, 1960

BC-5
Clear, 8oz., red and white ACL
Elf on left, Brownie Bottling Co.
Art deco, stippled rectangles
Glenshaw Glass Co.
Z on lip, 1954

BC-6
Clear, 8oz., red and white ACL
Elf on left, Blue Ribbon Bottling Co.
Art deco, stippled rectangles
Glenshaw Glass Co.
1958 (D on lip), 1959

BC-7
Clear, 8oz., red and white ACL
Elf on left, Blue Ribbon Bottling Co.
Art deco, diamond pattern
Glenshaw Glass Co.
1961, 1962

BC-8
Clear, 8oz., red and white ACL
Elf on left, Blue Ribbon Bottling Co.
Plain bottle
Anchor Hocking Glass Co.
1963

BC-9
Clear, 12oz., red and white ACL
Elf on front center, Brownie Bottling Co.
Brownie in block letters
No design (plain bottle)
Glenshaw Glass Co.
K and L on lips, 1939, 1940

BC-10
Clear, green, 28 fl. Oz., red and white ACL
Elf on front center, Brownie Bottling Co.

Brownie is in block letters, not script
Contents 1pt. 12 fl. Oz. embossed on heel
Glenshaw Glass Co.
1947, 48, Q?- 1945

BC-11
Clear, green, 28 fl. Oz., red and white ACL
Elf on front center, Brownie Bottling Co.
Art deco
Not sure?

BC-12
Green, 28 fl. Oz.,, red and white ACL
Elf on left side, Brownie Bottling Co. Inc.
Contents 1 Pt., 12 Fl. Oz. embossed
Brownie Club shoulder label is red
Glenshaw Glass Co,
V on neck, 1950

BC-13
Green and clear, 28oz., red and white ACL
Elf on left side, Brownie Bottling Co.
Contents 1pt. 12 fl. Oz embossed
Shoulder label is white
Glenshaw Glass Co.
1947 (Weide)

BC-14
Clear, Green, 28oz., red and white ACL
Elf on left side, Blue Ribbon Bottling Co.
Contents 1 Pt., 12 Fl. Oz. embossed
Glenshaw Glass Co.
D on neck, 1958, 1961

BC-15
Green, 1pt. 12 fl. Oz., red and white ACL
Elf on left side, Blue Ribbon Bottling Co.
Glenshaw Glass Co.
1964

Brownie Club Pale Dry Ginger Ale (scarce)
BC-16
Green, 7oz., white and red ACL
Elf on left
Brownie Club Bottling Co.
Glenshaw Glass Co.
1948

Canada Dry—Providence, RI (scarce)
CD-1
Green, 7oz., red and white ACL
Pale Dry Ginger Ale
Canada Dry Bottling Co.
No design
Owens Illinois Glass Co.
1948

Champagner—Riverside, RI (very rare)
CH-1
Green, 12oz., red and yellow ACL
Champagne glass on front
Riverside Bottling Co.
Glenshaw Glass Co.
ca. 1940-42

Clover Club Beverages—Providence, RI (semicommon)
CL-1
Clear, 7oz., white and green ACL
—may not exist?

CL-2
Clear, 8oz., white and green ACL
Clover Club Bottling Co.
Enriched with vitamin C (rear neck)
Anchor Hocking Glass Co.
1959

CL-3
Clear, 8oz., white and green ACL
Clover Club Bottling Co.
Enriched with vitamin (C) (rear neck)
C is in parenthesis
Anchor Hocking Glass Co.
1956

Cl-4
Clear, 8 oz., white and green ACL (uncommon)
Clover Club Bottling Co.
Fancy version, hollow clover and clover flower
Reed Glass Co.
1946, 47, 48

CL-5
Green, 7oz., red and white ACL (rare)
Clover Club Bottling Co.
Hollow clovers
Anchor Hocking Glass Co.
1959

Clover Club Pale Dry Ginger Ale—Providence, RI (rare)
CL-6
Green, 8oz., white and red ACL
Clovers on front, Pale Dry to left of Ginger Ale
Reed Glass Co.
1948

CL-7
Green, 7oz., white and red ACL
Clovers on front, Pale Dry above Ginger Ale
Anchor Hocking Glass Co.
1955
—info from second broken example

Clover Club Sparkling Water—Providence, RI (scarce)

CL-8
Clear, 7oz., white and blue ACL
Four leaf clover
Clover Club Bottling Co.
Anchor Hocking Glass Co.
1956

CL-9
Clear, 7oz., white and green ACL
Four leaf clover
Clover Club Bottling Co.
Anchor Hocking Glass Co.
1953

Coca-Cola—Newport, RI

CC-1
Aqua, 10oz., white ACL
Hobbleskirt, location embossed on base
Coca-Cola Bottling Co.
Illinois Glass Co.
1960-70s

CC-2
Aqua, 12oz., white ACL
Hobbleskirt, location embossed on base
Coca-Cola Bottling Co.
L?
1960-70s

CC-3
Aqua, 16oz., white ACL
Hobbleskirt, location on base, return for deposit on neck
L?
1980

Coca-Cola—Peace Dale, RI (scarce)

CC-4
Aqua, 6-1/2oz., white ACL
Hobbleskirt, location on base

CC-5
Aqua, 6-1/2oz., white ACL
Hobbleskirt, location on base, money back bottle/return for deposit on neck
Illinois Glass Co.?
1966

CC-6
Aqua, 12oz., white ACL
Illinois Glass Co.?
1968

CC-7
Aqua, 16oz, white ACL
Illinois Glass Co?
(check for 10oz. bottle)

Coca-Cola—Providence (common)

CC-8
Aqua, 6-1/2oz., white ACL

CC-9
Aqua, 10 fl. oz., white ACL
Illinois Glass Co.
Trademark and 10oz. separate

CC-10
Aqua, 10 fl. oz., white ACL
Trademark and 10oz. together
L

CC-11
Aqua, 10 fl. oz., white ACL
Money back bottle

CC-12
Aqua, 16oz., white ACL

CC-13
Aqua, 26oz., white ACL
Anchor Hocking Glass Co.
1972

CC-14
Aqua, 1pt. 10fl. Oz.
Anchor Hocking Glass Co.
1967

CC-15
Aqua, 32oz., white ACL

Cott Quality Beverages—Pawtucket, RI

CT-1
Clear, 7oz., white, red, and blue ACL
Rectangular label, house of Cott on shoulder
Cott Bottling Co. of RI

CT-2
Clear, 7oz., white, red, and black ACL
Shield crest, stars on shoulder
Stippled body
House of Cott is black
Cott Bottling Co. Inc.
Thatcher Glass Co.
1954

CT-3
Clear, 7oz., white, red, and black ACL
Shield crest, stars on shoulder
Stippled body
House of Cott is clear

Cott Bottling Co. of RI
Anchor Hocking Glass Co.
1957

CT-4
Green bottle, red, white, and black ACL
Shield crest, stars on shoulder
House of Cott is black
Cott Bottling Co. of RI
Owens Illinois Glass Co.
1953

Cott Quality—Pawtucket, RI (semicommon)
CT-5
Clear, 7 oz., red, white and blue ACL
House of Cott crest on shoulder (2x) and front
Front label is two overlaid ovals
Cott Beverage Corp. New Haven, Conn., Cott Bottling Co., RI
Entire body is stippled
Glenshaw Glass Co., Illinois Glass Co.
1960 Illinois, 61 Glenshaw

CT-6
Green, 7 oz., red and white ACL
House of Cott crest on shoulder (2x) and front
Plain bottle
Cott Beverage Corp. New Haven, Conn., Cott Bottling Co., RI
Glenshaw Glass Co.
1961

CT-7
Clear, 7oz., white and blue ACL
House of Cott crest on shoulder (2x) and front, return for refund

Front label is two overlaid ovals
Cott Bottling Co. of RI
Entire body is lightly stippled
Illinois Glass Co. (also Thatcher Glass Co.)
1965, (1966)

Cotton Club Beverages—Cranston, RI
CN-1
Clear, 8 fl. oz., red and white ACL (scarce)
Man conducting band on front, plain shoulders
The Sign of Quality, drink the best
Reed Glass Co.
1945, 47

CN-2
Clear, contents 8 fl. oz., red and white ACL (scarce)
Man conducting band on front, horizontal ribbed shoulders
Contents 8 Fluid Ounces embossed on base
Cotton Club Beverage Co.
Reed Glass Co.
1951

CN-3
Clear and green, quart, red and white ACL (clear uncommon, rare in green)
Man conducting band on front, horizontal ribbed shoulders
Cotton Club Beverage Co.
Reed Glass Co.
1946 clear, 1946, 1951 green

Daly Aid Pale Dry Ginger Ale—Central Falls, RI (rare)

DA-1
Green, 7oz., red and white ACL
Dexter Bottling Co.
Girl on fence
Glenshaw Glass Co.
1960

Deep Rock—W. Barrington, RI (scarce)
DR-1
Green, 8oz., yellow ACL
Art deco rectangles pattern
Deep Rock, 8oz., W. Barrington, R.I. embossed on base
Owens Illinois Glass Co.
1939

DR-2
Clear, 8oz., red ACL
Art deco rectangles pattern
Deep Rock, 8oz., W. Barrington, R.I. embossed on base
Owens Illinois Glass Co.
1937, 1938

Deep Rock Beverages—W. Barrington, RI (rare)
DR-3
Clear, quart, maroon and white ACL
Deep Rock Inc.
Big front label with two rectangles full of dots, Deep Rock on shoulder
Owens Illinois Glass Co.
1942

Dexter Beverages—Central Falls, RI (rare)
DX-1
Clear, 8 oz., red and white ACL
Well on front, Dexter serve cold on shoulder
Lightly stippled body

Dexter Bottling Co.
Glenshaw Glass Co.
1958?

DX-2
Clear, green, 1pt. 12 fl. oz., red and white ACL
Well on front, Dexter serve cold on shoulder
One pint 12 fl.ozs.
Dexter Bottling Co.
Glenshaw Glass Co.
1965 (clear), 1955?, 1965 green

DX-3
Clear, green, 1pt. 12 fl. oz., red and white ACL
Well on front, Dexter serve cold on shoulder
1 pint 12 fluid ounces
Dexter Bottling Co.
Glenshaw Glass Co.
19? (illegible date code)

DX-4
Clear, green, quart, red and white ACL
Well on front, lattice diamond pattern on shoulder
Dexter Bottling Co.
Glenshaw Glass Co.
1951 (green and clear)

Drink Me Pop—Woonsocket, RI (uncommon)
DM-1
Clear, 12oz., red and white ACL
Batchelor's Beverages Inc. 80 River St.
Shoulder ACLs, money back, modern
Glenshaw Glass Co.
1979

Dub-L-Valu—Bristol, RI (rare)
DV-1
Clear, 12oz., white and red ACL
Stippled heel and neck, band of dots on shoulder
5c for two glasses
Eagle Bottling Co. (embossed on base)
Reed Glass Co.
1940

DV-2
Clear, 12oz., white and red ACL
Stippled heel and neck, band of dots on shoulder
5c for two glasses
Eagle Bottling Co. (pyro on back)
Reed Glass Co.
1941

Drink E. J. Dybala Soda—Cranston, RI (semicommon)
DY-1
Clear and green, quart, red and white ACL
Shoulder ACL, art deco squares body
E.J. Dybala Bottling Works
Glenshaw Glass Co.
1956 or 1959, 1960

Enjoy E. J. Dybala Soda (rare)
DY-2
Clear, 32oz., red and white ACL
Taste the difference motto, horizontal ribs on shoulder
Reed Glass Co.
1956?

E. J. Dybala Beverages (rare)
DY-3
Green, 32oz., white and red ACL
Band silhouette, arched horizontal ribs on shoulder
E.J. Dybala Bottling Co.
Reed Glass Co.
1953

DY-4
Clear, 8oz., red and white ACL
Band silhouette, arched horizontal ribs on shoulder
E.J. Dybala Bottling Co.
Reed Glass Co.
1954

Dybala's Spring Beverages—Woonsocket, RI (scarce)
DS-1
Clear, 12oz., blue and white ACL
Picture of spring on front, stippled body
Dybalas Spring Bottling Works
Reed Glass Co.
194?

DS-2
Clear, green, 28oz., blue and white ACL
Embossed Dybala's Spring (2x)/ Capacity 28 Fl. Oz. Reg./ Woonsocket, RI
Dybala Spring Bottling Works
Picture of spring on front
Reed Glass Co.
1940, 1945, 47, 1950 (Clear, Weide), 1951 (green)

DS-3
Clear, green, 1pt. 12oz., red and white ACL (uncommon)
Dybala's Spring Bottling Works
Spring on front, plain bottle
Glenshaw Glass Co.
1966

Eagle Beverages—Bristol Rhode Island (rare)
EA-1
Clear, 28 fl oz., red and white ACL
Eagle in background, shoulder ACL
Eagle Bottling Co.
Reed Glass Co.
1946

EA-2
Clear, 7-1/2 fl. oz., red and white ACL
Eagle in background, stippled rectangles on shoulder and heel?
Eagle Bottling Co.
Reed Glass Co.
1950?

Echo Spring Beverages-Bristol, RI (very rare)
EC-1
Clear, 28oz., red and white ACL
Shouting man and mountain
Two rings around shoulder
Reed Glass Co.
1943, 1945

Empire Beverages—Bristol, RI (common)
EM-1
Clear, quart (1pt. 12oz.), red and white ACL
Crown design, white shoulder ACL
Modern bottle, oz. and ml on front
White shoulder logo
Glenshaw Glass Co.
1978, 1984

EM-2
Clear, quart (1pt. 12oz.), red and white ACL
Crown design, white shoulder ACL
Modern bottle, only oz. on front
Red shoulder logo
Glenshaw Glass Co.
1974

Empire Club Beverages—Bristol, RI (x-rare)
EM-3
Clear, quart (28oz), red and white ACL
Estate style house on front
Plain bottle
Empire Bottling Works
Reed Glass Co.
1952

EM-4
Clear, 12oz., red and white ACL
Estate style house on front
Stippled glass
Empire Bottling Works
Reed Glass?

Frisky Lithiated Lemon Beverage (uncommon)
FY-1
Green, 7oz., red and white ACL
No town, but there was a Frisky Bottling Co. of RI in Providence (also one in CT)
Glenshaw Glass Co.
1947, 48

Frostie Root Beer—Centredale, RI (scarce)
FR-1
Clear, 12oz., cream ACL
Yacht Club Bottling Co.
Stippled neck, shoulder, and heel
A Real Taste Treat, you'll love it!
Owens Illinois Glass Co.
1951, 53?

Girard Spring Water—No. Providence, RI (uncommon)
GS-1
Green, 32oz., white ACL
Girard Spring Water Co. Inc., 1100 Mineral Spring Ave.
Plain bottle
One Full Quart embossed on base
Glenshaw Glass Co.
1948?

GS-2
Green, 32oz., white ACL
Girard Spring Water Co. Inc., 1100 Mineral Spring Ave.
Plain bottle
Contents one quart on front
Glenshaw Glass Co.
1960s

Glee Club Beverages—Providence, RI (all rare)
GC-1
Green, 7oz., red and white ACL
Girl dancing and musical notes, Glee Club on shoulder

Glee Club Beverages
Glenshaw Glass Co.

GC-2
Clear, 8oz., red and white ACL
Girl dancing and musical notes, Glee Club on shoulder

GC-3
Clear, 8oz., red and white ACL
Art deco paneled heel and shoulders
Glenshaw Glass Co.
1941, 1944

GC-4
Green, clear, 32oz., red and white ACL
Girl dancing and musical notes, Glee Club on shoulder
Glenshaw Glass Co.
1947

GC-5
Clear, 12oz., red and white ACL
Girl dancing and musical notes, Glee Club on shoulder

Grandpa's Draft Type New England Style Beverages—Providence, RI (rare)
GR-1
Clear, 64oz., red and white ACL
Barrel on front (left side), return bottle for refund
Stippled body
Brownie Bottling Co.
1950s, pre-1956

GR-2
Clear, 64oz., red and white ACL
Barrel on front (left side), every bottle sterilized
Stippled body
Brownie Bottling Co.
1940s-1956

Hebe—Providence (very rare)
HE-1
Clear, 28oz., red and white ACL
Hebe goddess, pillars
The Hebe Co.
Reed Glass Co.
1942

Hope Club Sparkling Beverages Cranston, RI (15 w. colors) (very common)
HC-1
Clear, 7oz., red and white ACL
Plain bottle, scroll label, shoulder label
Return for deposit on rear shoulder
Glenshaw Glass Co.
1975

HC-2
Green, 7oz., red and white ACL
Plain bottle, scroll label
Illinois Glass Co.
1960 or 69

HC-3
Clear, 8oz., red and white ACL
Art deco rectangular design, scroll label
Illinois Glass Co.
1968

HC-4
Clear, 8oz., red and white ACL
Deco, horizontal circles on neck and heel, scroll label
Illinois Glass Co.
1970 or 1978

HC-5
Clear, 8oz., red and white ACL
Deco, horizontal circles on neck and heel, scroll label
Return for deposit
Illinois Glass Co.
1972

HC-6
Clear, 8oz., red and white ACL
Stippled neck, money back bottle return for deposit on shoulder
Illinois Glass Co.
1973

HC-7
Clear and green, 28oz., red and white ACL
Wine glass, lemon front
Plain bottle
Illinois Glass Co.
1970

HC-8
Green and clear, quart, red and white ACL
Wine glass, lemon front
Money back bottle on rear shoulder
Plain bottle
Illinois Glass Co.
1972?

HC-9
Clear, 28oz., red and white ACL
Scroll label, stippled body

Money back bottle on rear shoulder
Glenshaw Glass Co.
1975

Hope Club Sparkling Beverages Providence, RI
HC-10
Green and clear, 8 oz., red and white ACL
Art deco rectangular design, scroll label
Illinois Glass Co.
1961, 62 clear, 1955, 1961 green

HC-11
Clear, green, quart, red and white ACL
Hope Club Beverages on shoulder, wine glass, lemon shape on front, Hope Club embossed on shoulder (white ACL only)
Reed Glass Co.
1943 clear, 1945 green

HC-12
Clear, green, quart, red and white ACL
Hope Club Beverages on shoulder, wine glass, lemon shape on front, Hope Club embossed on shoulder (white and red ACL)
Owens Illinois Glass Co. (1950s), Illinois Glass Co. 1960s
1956, 57 clear, 1965, 1969 green

Ideal Beverages—Central Falls, RI (scarce)
ID-1
Clear, 8oz., red and white ACL
House and rolling hills
Art deco vertical ribs on shoulder
Ideal Beverage Co.
Reed Glass Co.
1946

ID-2
Clear, 32oz, red and white ACL
House and rolling hills on front, Ideal Beverages on shoulder
Ideal Beverage Co.
Reed Glass Co.
1943, 45, 1947

Kerona Beverages—Central Falls, RI (uncommon)
KB-1
Clear, 1 pt. 12oz., blue and white ACL
Deep Rock Spring on shoulder, The K Co. on front. No back ACL
REGISTERED embossed on front heel
Reed Glass Co.
1948

KB-2
Green, 1pt. 12oz., red and white ACL
Deep Rock Spring on shoulder, The K Co. on front. No back ACL
REGISTERED embossed on front heel
Reed Glass Co.
1944, 1946

King Orange Soda—W. Barrington, RI (rare)
KO-1
Clear, 12oz., blue and white ACL
Deep Rock Inc.
Crown and shield, semi-squat, flower-ish design on shoulder and heel
Owens Illinois Glass Co.
1941

Korker—Graniteville, RI (very rare)
KR-1
Green, 7oz., white and yellow ACL
Bare Rock Beverage Co.
Plain bottle, A corking good drink
Owens Illinois Glass Co.
1940

Lambert's Delicious Carbonated Beverages—Woonsocket, RI (semicommon)
LA-1
Clear, green, 7oz., red and white ACL
B., L., & M. Bottling Co.
Mountain on front, Lamberts on shoulder
Glenshaw Glass Co. (clear)
Reed Glass Co. (green)
1956, 57, 59 (clear) 1954 (green)

LA-2
Clear, 7oz., green and white ACL (green scarce)
Lambert Bottling Co.
Oil City Glass Co.
pre-1953

Lambert's Delicious Carbonated Beverages—Woonsocket, RI (uncommon)
LA-3
Aqua, 7oz., green and white ACL

Different mountain style
1940

Ledge Brand Beverages Ochee—Providence, RI (clear scarce, green rare)

LG-1
Clear, green, 28oz., red and white ACL
Indian on shoulder (white ACL)
Ochee Spring Water Co.
Reed Glass Co.
1943, 45

LG-2
Clear, 28oz., red and white ACL
Indian on shoulder (red ACL)
Ochee Spring Water Co.

Liberty Beverages—Providence, RI (ex rare)

LB-1
Clear, 8oz, red and white ACL
Liberty bell on front
Plain body, shoulder and heel bulge out slightly
Bell Bottling Co.
?

Liberty Club Beverages—Providence, RI (common clear, scarce green)

LC-1
Clear, green, 8 oz., red and white ACL
House with two champagne glasses on front,
Supreme Mineral Water Co.
Glenshaw Glass Co.
1943 (green), 1942, 1946, 1954
Green is rare

Note: One example appears to have a white and reddish-orange ACL. We have not decided if this is to be considered a new version yet.

LC-2
Green, 7oz., red and white ACL
House with two champagne glasses on front
Supreme Mineral Water Co.
Glenshaw Glass Co.
S on lip, 1947

LC-3
Clear, 12oz., red and white ACL (scarce)
House with two champagne glasses on front
Stippled shoulder and neck
Glenshaw Glass Co.
K, 1939? seems too old

LC-4
Clear, 12oz., white and green ACL (possibly)
House with two champagne glasses on front
Stippled shoulder and neck
-found in marsh, could not find it the next day, but def. green looking

Lime-Up Beverage Mixer—Providence, RI (scarce)

LU-1
Green, 7oz., red and white ACL
Lime-Up on shoulder, sparkling beverage and mixer
Liberty Club Beverages
Glenshaw Glass Co.
T on lip, 1948

LU-2
Green, quart, red and white ACL
—may not exist

Ma's Old Fashion—Woonsocket, RI (very rare)

MA-1
Clear, 7oz., red and white ACL
Old Fashioned embossed on shoulder
Ma's Old Fashion Bottling Co.
Glenshaw Glass Co.
1957

Manhattan Beverages—Esmond, RI (rare)

MN-1
Clear, 12oz., yellow and red ACL
Entire body has horizontal ribs, shoulder label
Manhattan Beverages
Reed Glass Co.
1943

MN-2
Clear, Green, 32 fl. Oz., red and white ACL
Bottled by Manhattan Beverages
Swirled ribs on shoulder, neck
Esmond, RI embossed on base
Reed Glass Co.
1941 (both colors)

Manhattan Beverages—of Rhode Island (10) (Semicommon)

MN-3
Clear, 8oz., red and white ACL
Manhattan skyline, white shoulder ACL

Manhattan Bott. Co.
Plain bottle
Reed Glass Co.
1945

MN-4
Clear, 8oz., red and white ACL
Manhattan skyline, Red shoulder ACL
Manhattan Bott. Co.
Plain bottle
Reed Glass Co.
194?

MN-5
Clear, 12oz., yellow and red ACL
Entire body has horizontal ribs, shoulder label
Manhattan Beverages of RI
Reed Glass Co.
1944

MN-6
Clear, green, 32oz., red and white ACL
Manhattan skyline,
Manhattan Bott. Co.
Swirled ribs on shoulder and neck
Mahnattan Bottling Co. of R.I. embossed on base
Reed Glass Co.
1945 clear, 1944 green

Manhattan Beverages—Woonsocket, RI (common)
MN-7
Clear and green, 7 oz., red and white ACL
Manhattan skyline, round shoulder ACL
Plain bottle
1960-1971

MN-8
Green, 28oz., red and white ACL
Manhattan skyline- is this Toms?

MN-9
Clear, 28oz., red and white ACL
Manhattan skyline, serve cold on neck
Money back bottle, stippled shoulders
M & M Bottling Works, Inc.
Glenshaw Glass Co.
1978

MN-10
Clear, green, 1pt. 12fl. Oz., red and white ACL
Manhattan skyline
Serve Cold (shield) on neck
Glenshaw Glass Co.
1973

Martin's Beverages—Woonsocket, RI (scarce)
MR-1
Clear, Green, 28oz., red and white ACL
Keystone shaped front label, drink a preferred product
Martins Soda Works
Reed Glass Co.?
1949 (green), 1947

Mission of California—Woonsocket, RI (scarce)
MI-1
Clear, 7oz., blue and white ACL
Swirled ribs on shoulder, Spanish mission on front
Mission Orange Bottling Co.
Glenshaw Glass Co.
1958

MI-2
Clear, 7oz., blue and white ACL
Swirled ribs on shoulder
Mission Orange Bottling Co.
Glenshaw Glass Co.
1960 or 1968

MI-3
Clear, 7oz., blue and white ACL
Swirled ribs on shoulder, return for refund
Mission Orange Bottling Co.
Glenshaw Glass Co.
1967

MI-4
Clear, 7oz., blue and white ACL
plain bottle, return for refund
Mission Orange Bottling Co.
Glenshaw Glass Co.
1969

Mission Beverages—Woonsocket, RI (scarce)
MI-5
Clear, 7oz., black and white ACL
Swirled ribs on shoulder
Mission Orange Bottling Co.
Glenshaw Glass Co.
1955

MI-6
Green, 7oz., white ACL
Swirled ribs on shoulder
Mission Orange Bottling Co.
Glenshaw Glass Co.
Y=1953

Moose Head Beverages—Providence, RI (rare)

MH-1
Clear, 8oz., red and white ACL
Moose head on front, vertical ribs on shoulders
Moose Head Beverages
Glenshaw Glass Co.
1945, 46

MH-2
Clear, 8oz., red and white ACL
Moose head on front, vertical ribs on shoulder
Telephone Gaspee 8538
This bottle worth 2c at the store (back)
Reed Glass Co.
1943

MH-3 (very rare in green)
Clear and green, quart, red and white ACL
Shoulder ACL
Telephone Gaspee 8538
This bottle worth 5c at the store (back)
Reed Glass Co.
1941

MH-4
Clear, quart, red and white ACL
No shoulder ACL
Telephone Gaspee 8538
Reed Glass Co.?

Nehi Beverages—Providence, RI (semicommon)
NE-1
Clear, 9-1/2", 12oz., red and yellow ACL
Normal art deco design
Royal Crown Bottling Co. of RI
Des. Pat. # embossed on base
Thatcher Glass Co.
1950, 1952

Newport Club Beverages—Newport, RI (rare)
NC-1
Clear, green, 6oz., red and white ACL
Navigation buoy on front, art deco shoulders, Newport Club on shoulder
Coca-Cola Bottling Co. of Newport
Illinois Glass Co. (Clear)
Chattanooga Glass Co. (green)
1955 clear

Nugget, Good As Gold—Providence, RI (common)
NU-1
Clear, 12 oz., black and white ACL
Gold nugget on front
Red Fox Ginger Ale Co.
1944 printed date
Reed Glass Co.
1944, 45

NU-2
Clear, 12 oz., black and white ACL
Gold nugget on front
Red Fox Ginger Ale Co.
No printed date
Glenshaw Glass Co.
19?

NU-3
Clear, 12oz., black and white ACL
Gold nugget on front
Red Fox Ginger Ale Co.
Printed date, orange drink on back
Thatcher Glass Co., Glenshaw Glass Co.
1948 Thatcher, 1960, 61 66 Glenshaw

Ochee Beverages—Providence, RI (10) (semicommon, green scarce)
OC-1
Clear, green, 8oz., black and white ACL
Indian and Est. 1875 on shoulder (2x), bubbles on front
The Water of Quality
Capacity on front
Ochee Spring Water Co.
Reed Glass Co.
1940, 1944, 1947

OC-2
Clear, 8oz., black and white ACL (uncommon)
Indian and Est. 1875 on shoulder (2x), bubbles on front
No capacity (oz.) on bottle
Reed Glass Co.
1943
Thatcher Glass Co.
1948

OC-3
Clear, 28oz., black and white ACL (uncommon)
Indian and Est. 1875 on shoulder (2x), bubbles on front
Reed Glass Co.
1945, 47

OC-4
Clear, 32oz., black and white ACL (uncommon)
Indian and Est. 1875 on shoulder (2x), bubbles on front
stippled body
Reed Glass Co.
1945

OC-5
Clear, 1pt. 12 fl. oz., black and white ACL
Indian and Est. 1875 on shoulder (2x), bubbles on front
Registered in ACL on back, stippled body
Thatcher Glass Co.
1948

Ochee Club Soda—Providence, RI (rare)
OC-6
Clear, 7oz., black and white ACL
Indian and Est. 1875 on shoulder, bubbles on front
Reed Glass Co.
1944, 48

OC-7
Clear, 32oz., black and white ACL
Indian and Est. 1875 on shoulder, bubbles on front
Reed Glass Co.?

Ochee Pale Dry Ginger Ale—Providence, RI (scarce clear, rare green)
OC-8
Clear, green, 8oz., black and white ACL
Indian and Est. 1875 on shoulder, bubbles on front
Ochee Spring Water Co.
Reed Glass Co.
1945

OC-9
Green, 7oz., black and white ACL
Stippled body
Ochee Spring Water Co.
Reed Glass Co.
1945

OC-10
Clear, 32oz., black and white ACL
Small Indian
1945 (might be the same as OC-8)

OC-11
Green, 32oz., black and white ACL
Indian and Est. 1875 on shoulder, bubbles on front
Ochee Spring Water Co., Ochee embossed on heel plain bottle
Reed Glass Co.
1943 or 48

OC-12
Green, 32oz., black and white ACL
Indian and Est. 1875 on shoulder, bubbles on front
Ochee Spring Water Co., 32 Fl. Oz. embossed on base
stippled body
Reed Glass Co.
1946

Old English Beverages—Central Falls, RI (Scarce)
OE-1
Clear, 7oz., blue and white ACL
Crest with lions, shoulder label
The Kerona Co.
Glenshaw Glass Co.
1962, 63

Pepsi-Cola—West Warwick, RI (8) (uncommon)
PC-1
Clear, 12oz., red, white, and blue ACL
Double dot, double dot on neck
West Warwick below shoulder
Owens Illinois Glass Co.
1948

PC-2
Clear, 12oz., red, white, and blue ACL
Double dot, single dot on neck
West Warwick below shoulder
Owens Illinois Glass Co.
1948

PC-3
Clear, 12oz., red, white, and blue ACL
Double dot
West Warwick near heel
19

PC-4
Clear, 8oz., red and white ACL
Double dot, double dot on neck
Pepsi-Cola Bottling Co. of RI
Anchor Hocking Glass Co.
19

Pepsi-Cola—West Warwick, RI (common)
PC-5
Clear, 12oz., blue, red, and white ACL
Single dot
West Warwick written twice (on neck and shoulder) (check others)
Owens Illinois Glass Co.
1952

PC-6
Clear, 8oz., red and white ACL
Single dot
Try Our Economy size
Anchor Hocking Glass Co.
1953

PC-7
Clear, 8oz., red and white ACL
Single dot
Franchised bottler
Anchor Hocking Glass Co.
1942? (no), 1957?

PC-8
Clear, 12oz., red and white ACL
Single dot
West Warwick on neck and shoulder
Pepsi-Cola Bottling Co. of RI Inc.
Des. Pat. 120,277 on base
Illinois Glass Co.
1954, 56, 57

PC-9
Clear, 12oz., red and white ACL
Single dot
West Warwick on neck and shoulder
Pepsi-Cola Bottling Co.
Des. Pat. 120,277 on base
Owens Illinois Glass Co.
1953?

Pepsi-Cola Fountain Syrup—W. Warwick, RI (rare)
PC-10
Clear, 12oz., red and white ACL
Double dot
Fountain Syrup written on front shoulder and front of bottle, directions on back
Pepsi-Cola Bottling Co.
Owens Illinois Glass Co.

Beverages by Red Fox—Providence, RI (common)
RF-1
Clear and green, 7oz., red and white ACL
Fox head on shoulder
Red Fox Ginger Ale Co.
Glenshaw Glass Co. (green)
1970 green, 1951 clear

RF-2
Clear and green, 7oz., red and white ACL
Fox head on shoulder, return for deposit on back, zip code
Red Fox Ginger Ale Co.
Glenshaw Glass Co.
1976 clear, 1978 green

Red Fox Pale Ginger Ale—Providence, RI
RF-3
Green, 7oz, red and white ACL
Red Fox Ginger Ale Co.
Reed Glass Co.
1951

Red Fox Super Saturated Club Soda—Providence, RI (semicommon)
RF-4
Clear, 7oz., white and blue ACL
Fox on shoulder, bubbles on front
7oz. on front and back
Glenshaw Glass Co.
1961, 1967

RF-5
Clear, 7oz., white and blue ACL
Fox on shoulder, bubbles on front
7oz. only on back
Glenshaw Glass Co.
1960

Enjoy Red Rock Cola—Red Rock of RI (scarce)
RR-1
Clear, 12oz., red and white ACL
Red Rock Cola on shoulder
Red Rock Bottling Co. of RI
Reed Glass Co.
1944

RR-2
Clear, 7oz., red and white ACL
Enjoy the sparkling rich flavor of... (back)
Red Rock Bottling Co. of RI
Thatcher Glass Co.
19?

Ritz-E Sparkling Beverages—Providence, RI (uncommon)
RZ-1
Green, clear, salt/pepper shaker size (5-1/2"), red and white ACL (rare)
Bell Bottling Co., Inc.
Screw cap with metal shaker top
Glenshaw Glass Co.

RZ-2
Clear, 12 oz., white and blue ACL
Ritz-E Beverages on shoulder
Bell Bottling Co.

Glenshaw Glass Co.
1940, 42, 1949

RZ-3
Clear, 28oz., white and blue ACL
Ritz-E Beverages on shoulder
Bell Bottling Co.
Glenshaw Glass Co.
1942

RZ-4
Clear, green, 28 fl. Oz., red and white ACL
Bell Bottling Co., Inc
Glenshaw Glass Co.
1949, 1950 clear, 1944 green

Rose—Johnston, RI (7) (common)

RO-1
Clear, green, 7 oz., red and white ACL
Rose on front, Est. 1910 on back
The Family Beverage
Rose Beverage Co.
Illinois Glass Co.
1964, 66 clear 1967 green

RO-2
Clear, green, 1pt. 12oz., red and white ACL
Rose on front, no zip code
The Family Beverage
Rose Beverage Co.
Contents 1pt. 12 fl. Oz. embossed on base
Illinois Glass Co.
1966, 68 (clear), 1967 (green)

RO-3
Clear, 1pt. 12oz., red and white ACL
Rose on front, Est. 1910 and zip code on front, back
The Family Beverage
Rose Beverage Co.
Illinois Glass Co.
1971

Rose—Providence, RI (common, green semi-common)

RO-4
Clear, green, 7oz, red and white ACL
Rose on front
The Family Beverage
Thatcher Glass Co.
1951, 1964 (clear), 1964 (green)

RO-5
Green, 1pt. 12oz., red and white ACL
Rose on front
The Family Beverage
Rose Beverage Co.
Contents 1pt. 12 fl. Oz. embossed on base
Owens Illinois Glass Co.
195?, 1959, 1963

RO-6
Clear, 1pt. 12oz., red and white ACL
Rose on front
The Family Beverage
Rose Beverage Co.
Contents 1pt. 12 fl. Ozs. embossed on heel
Thatcher Glass Co.
1959

Royal Crown Cola—Providence, RI (semicommon)

RC-1
Aqua, 12oz., red and yellow ACL
Pyramid label
Owens Illinois Glass Co.
1945

RC-2
Clear, 12oz., red and yellow ACL (rare)
Pyramid label
Glenshaw Glass Co.
1940s?

RC-2
Aqua, 12oz., red and yellow ACL (uncommon)
Pyramid label, Good Housekeeping Bureau seal on back
Owens Illinois Glass Co.
1940

7-Up—Middletown, RI (semicommon)

SU-1
Green, 7oz., red and white ACL (uncommon)
Bubble girl
Seven Up Bottling Co.
Glenshaw Glass Co.
1947

SU-2
Green, 7oz., red and white ACL
Bubble girl
Seven Up Newport Bottling Co.
Glenshaw Glass Co.
1946

SU-3
Green, 7oz., red and white ACL
Bubble girl
Seven Up Bottling Co. of Southern RI
Glenshaw Glass Co.
1947

SU-4
Green, 7oz., red and white ACL
Bubbles
No design

7-Up—West Barrington, RI (semicommon)
SU-5
Green, 7oz., red and white ACL
Bubble girl
You like it, it likes you
Seven Up Bottling Co., West Barrington
Glenshaw Glass Co.
1946, 1947

SU-6
Green, 7oz., red and white ACL
Bubble girl, Seven-Up on back lower shoulder
You like it, it likes you
Seven Up Bottling Co., W. Barrington (abbreviated)
Owens Illinois Glass Co.
1948

SU-7
Green, 7oz., red and white ACL
Bubbles, shoulder label
You like it, it likes you
Seven Up Bottling Co.
Glenshaw Glass Co., Anchor Hocking Glass Co.
1953 Glenshaw, 1957 Anchor

SU-8
Green, 12oz., red and white ACL
Bubbles, shoulder label
Fresh Up with 7-Up (neck),
You like it, it likes you
Seven Up Bottling Co.

Anchor Hocking Glass Co., Glenshaw Glass Co.
1960 G, 1963 AH

SU-9
Green, 1pt. 12oz., red and white ACL
Bubbles, shoulder labels
You Like it, it likes you
Seven Up Bottling Co.

Seacrest Beverages—Bristol, RI (rare)
SE-1
Clear, 7oz., cream and black ACL (possibly white)
Lighthouse w. clouds, ocean on front
Stippled body
United Bottling Works
Reed Glass Co.?
1948

SE-2
Clear, 1pt. 12 fl. oz., white and black ACL
Lighthouse w. clouds, ocean on front
United Bottling Works
Thatcher Glass Co.
1948, 1951

Shiloh Beverages—Providence, RI (rare)
SH-1
Clear, 9 oz., red and white ACL
Shiloh on shoulder, Indian on front, rectangular label
Shiloh Bottling Co.
Reed Glass Co.
1948

SH-2
Clear, 9oz., red and white ACL
Solid headdress, arched label top
Shiloh Bottling Co.

SH-3
Clear, 9oz., red and white ACL
Shiloh in 3-D block letters, headdress not solid, arched label top
Shiloh Bottling Co.

Simba—no town (semicommon)
SI-1
Green, 10oz., red, white, and yellow ACL
White lion on body
The Coca-Cola Company
1968

SI-2
Green, 10oz., white ACL
Lion on body, screw cap
The Coca-Cola Company
Illinois Glass Co.
1968

South County Beverages—Peace Dale, RI (2) (semicommon)
SC-1
Clear, 6oz., red and white ACL
Octagon shaped label with bubbles
Coca-Cola Bottling Co.
Owens Illinois (1951), Anchor Hocking (1959)
1951, 1959

SC-2
Green, 26oz., red and white ACL (rare)
Octagon shaped label with bubbles

Coca-Cola Bottling Co.
Illinois Glass Co.
1956

Drink Speedball—West Warwick, RI (uncommon)
SB-1
Clear, 12 oz., Blue, orange and white ACL
Rings around neck
It Sings in the Glass (rear shoulder)
Orange baseball, drink is straight
Warwick Club Ginger Ale Co.
Glenshaw Glass Co.
Y on lip= 1953, 1966?

SB-2
Clear, 12 oz., Blue, orange and white ACL (rare)
Rings around neck
It Sings in the Glass (rear shoulder)
Orange baseball, drink is arched up
Glenshaw Glass Co.
1948

SB-3
Clear, 12oz., red, white, and blue ACL (scarce)
Rings around neck
It Sings in the Glass
Red baseball, drink is straight
Warwick Club Ginger Ale Co. Inc.
Glenshaw Glass Co.
1962

Spike-It—Providence, RI
SK-1
Amber, 7oz., yellow and black ACL (very rare)
You'll Like It, bubbles on front

Red Fox Ginger Ale Co.
Reed Glass Co.
1941

Spur Canada Dry—Providence, RI (uncommon)
SP-1
Aqua, 12oz., red and white ACL (uncommon)
Zip In Every Sip
Ochee Spring Water Company
Spur on back shoulder too
Owens Illinois Glass Co.
1941

SP-2
Clear, 12oz., red and white ACL (uncommon)
A Cola Beverage, Ochee Spring Water Company
Reed Glass Co.
1943

SP-3
Clear, 28oz., red and white ACL
Registered embossed on heel, no design
A Cola Beverage, Reg. US Pat. Off.
Bottled and manufactured by Ochee Spring Water Co.
Reed Glass Co.
1944

SP-4
Clear, 28oz., red and white ACL
Registered embossed on heel, no design
A Cola Beverage, Trademark Reg.
Bottled and manufactured by Ochee Spring Water Co.

Reed Glass Co.
1943

Squirt—Providence, RI (semicommon)
SQ-1
Green, 7oz., red and yellow ACL
Large spiral grip-like ribs
Squirt Bottling Co. (Co. underneath T of fancy Squirt)
Glenshaw Glass Co.
1963, 64

SQ-1a
Green, 7oz., red and yellow ACL
Large spiral grip-like ribs
Squirt Bottling Co. (Co centered under fancy Squirt)
Glenshaw Glass Co.
1958

Squirt of Rhode Island (scarce)
SQ-2
Green, 7oz., red and yellow ACL
Plain bottle
Squirt Bottling Co. of Rhode Island
Reed Glass Co.
1944

Star Sparkling Beverages, Pawtucket, RI (scarce)
ST-1
Clear, 12oz., red and white ACL
Shoulder label
Star Bottling Co. Inc.
1940

ST-2
Clear, 28oz., white and green ACL

Plain bottle
Contents 1pt. 12 fl. oz. embossed on base
Star Bottling Co. Inc.
Reed Glass Co.
1948

ST-3
Green, 28oz., white and green ACL
Plain bottle
Star Bottling Co. Inc.
Reed Glass Co.
1942

Dr. Swett's (Original) Root Beer—West Barrington, RI (scarce)

SW-1
Clear, 9-1/2", 12oz., red and yellow ACL
From Childhood to Old Age motto, Dr. Swett's Original Root Beer on neck
Young boy and old man drinking from a glass
Stippled upper neck, horizontal ribs on shoulder
Embossed Contents 12 Fl. Oz. Registered on heel and Ss on shoulder
Deep Rock Inc.
Owens Illinois Glass Co.
1940 (45?)

SW-2
Clear, 12oz., red and yellow ACL
Dr. Swett's Root Beer w. Dextrose on neck
Large art deco S on front
Stippled upper neck, horizontal ribs on shoulder
Embossed Contents 12 Fl. Oz. Registered on heel and Ss on shoulder
Deep Rock Inc.
Owens Illinois Glass Co.
1942

SW-3
Clear, 28oz., red and yellow ACL
From childhood to old age motto, Dr. Swett's Original Root Beer on neck
Stippled upper neck, horizontal rings around shoulder
Dr. Swett's embossed on base, Ss on shoulder, 1pt. 12 fl. oz. Embossed on heel
Deep Rock Inc.
Owens Illinois Glass Co.
1940

Town Club Sparkling Beverages—Middletown, RI (scarce)

TC-1
Clear, green, 32oz., red and white ACL
Many vertical ribs on shoulder/neck area
Town Club Beverage Co.
This bottle is worth 5c at the store (on back), small "town" scene on front
Reed Glass Co.
1948 (clear), 1946? (green)

TC-2
Clear, 7oz., red and white ACL (rare)
stippled body, wide horizontal ribs on neck/shoulder
Reed Glass Co.
1948

Tru-Ade —West Barrington, RI (semicommon)

TA-1
Clear, 6-1/2oz., red and white ACL
Spaced vertical ribs with circles in between them on shoulders
Pasteurized, not carbonated in red circle
Tru-Ade Bottling Co., West Barrington
® on front
Thatcher Glass Co. (on one example)
1953

TA-2
Clear, 6-1/2oz., red and white ACL
Spaced vertical ribs with circles in between them on shoulders
Pasteurized, not carbonated in red circle
Tru-Ade Bottling Co., W. Barrington
® on front
Owens Illinois Glass Co., Anchor Hocking Glass Co.
1951 (Owens), 1953 (Anchor)

TA-3
Clear, 6-1/2oz., red and white ACL
Spaced vertical ribs with circles in between them on shoulders
Pasteurized, not carbonated, Tru-Ade on shoulder
Not carbonated below red circle
Tru-Ade Bottling Co.
Glenshaw Glass Co.
1963

TA-4
Clear, 7oz., red and white ACL
Spaced vertical ribs with circles in between them on shoulders
Reg. US Pat Off on front
Tru-Ade Bottling Co. of RI
Glenshaw Glass Co.
N on neck- 1942, U- 1949

TA-5
Clear, 7oz., red and white ACL
Spaced vertical ribs with circles in between them on shoulders
Reg. US Pat Off on front, 15% fruit juice
Tru-Ade Bottling Co. of RI
Owens Illinois Glass Co.
1942

TA-6
Clear, 10oz., red and white ACL
King Size on shoulder (2x)
Spaced vertical ribs with circles in between them on shoulders
Not carbonated in red circle
Tru-Ade Bottling Co.
Glenshaw Glass Co.
1955

TA-7
Clear, 10oz., red and white ACL
Tru-Ade King Size on shoulder (1x)
Spaced vertical ribs with circles in between them on shoulders
Not carbonated below red circle
Tru-Ade Bottling Co.
Glenshaw Glass Co.
1959

TA-8
Clear, 10oz., red and white ACL
Tru-Ade on shoulder in oval (2x)
Spaced vertical ribs with circles in between them on shoulders
Not carbonated below red circle
Glenshaw Glass Co.
1963, 65

TA-9
Clear, 10oz., red and white ACL
Tru-Ade on shoulder in small circle (2x)
Spaced vertical ribs with circles in between them on shoulders
Not carbonated in red circle
Tru-Ade Bottling Co.
Thatcher Glass Co.
1955

TA-10
Clear, 10oz., red and white ACL
Tru Ade on shoulder in oval (fancy version) (2x)
Spaced vertical ribs with circles in between them on shoulders
Not carbonated below red circle
Glenshaw Glass Co.
1962

Tweed Beverages—Providence, RI (x-rare)

TD-1
Clear, 12oz., blue and white ACL
Draped horizontal ribs on shoulder, stippled body
Lobello Spring Water Soda Co.
Reed Glass Co.
1944

Twin City Beverages, Central Falls, RI (scarce)

TW-1
Clear, 8 oz., red and white ACL
Stippled neck and shoulder, ACL stars
Neck label on front and back
Twin City Spring Beverage Co.
Anchor Hocking Glass Co.
1950

TW-2
Clear, 1pt. 12oz., red and white ACL
Stippled body, ACL stars
Twin City Spring Beverage Co.
Anchor Hocking Glass Co.
1949

Twin City Ginger Ale—Central Falls, RI

TW-3
Green, 28oz., brown and white ACL
Twin City Spring Beverage Co.
1949

Virginia Dare Beverages—Bristol, RI (12) (semicommon)

VD-1
Clear, 7oz., red and cream yellow ACL
Virginia Dare on shoulder, girl's head on front
Stippled body
Eagle Bottling Co.
Glenshaw Glass Co.
1958

VD-2
Clear, 7oz., red and cream yellow ACL
Virginia Dare on shoulder, girl's head on front
Stippled body, 7oz. On front of bottle
Eagle Bottling Co.
Glenshaw Glass Co.
1966

VD-3
Clear, 1pt. 12 fl. Oz., Red and cream yellow ACL
Virginia Dare on shoulder, girl's head on front
Eagle Bottling Co.
Stippled body, capacity written twice on front in two forms
Glenshaw Glass Co.
1975

VD-4
Clear, One pt. 12 fl. Oz., Red and cream yellow ACL
Virginia Dare on shoulder, girl's head on front
Eagle Bottling Co.
Stippled body, capacity written once on front with One pint spelled out
Glenshaw Glass Co.
1969

VD-5
Green, 1pt. 12 fl. oz., red and cream yellow ACL
Virginia Dare on shoulder, girl's head on front
Eagle Bottling Co.
Stippled body, capacity on back
Glenshaw Glass Co.
1965

VD-6
Clear, 12oz., red and cream yellow ACL (prove?)

Virginia Dare Beverages—Graniteville, RI (uncommon)

VD-7
Clear, oz., red and cream yellow ACL (prove?)

VD-8
Clear, 7oz., blue and white ACL
Plain bottle
Bare Rock Beverages
Owens Illinois Glass Co.
1944, 1953

VD-9
Clear, Green, 12oz., blue and white label
VD on shoulder
Bare Rock Beverage Co.
Illinois Glass Co.
1954 clear, 1960 green

VD-10
Clear, 12oz., blue and white label
Bare Rock Beverage Co.
12oz. embossed on shoulder
Owens Illinois Glass Co.
1945?

VD-11
Green, 1pt. 12fl. Oz., blue and white ACL
Plain body, capacity embossed on base
Quality beverages, serve cold
Bare Rock Beverage Co.
Owens Illinois Glass Co.
1954

VD-12
Clear, 1pt. 12 fl. Oz., blue and white ACL
Stippled body w. ring of small Xs on neck
Quality beverages, serve cold
Bare Rock Beverage Co.
Owens Illinois Glass Co.
1954?

VD-13
Clear, green, quart, blue and white ACL
Plain body
Bare Rock Beverage Co.
Virginia Dare on shoulder is in a slight double arch
Chill thoroughly for a delightful drink
Owens Illinois Glass Co.
1945 (clear), 1948 (green)

Virginia Dare Beverages—Johnston, RI (uncommon)

VD-14
Clear, 1pt. 12fl. Oz., white and blue ACL
Plain body
Quality beverages, serve cold
Bare Rock Beverage Co.
Illinois Glass Co.
1961

VD-15
Clear, 1pt. 12 fl. Oz., white and blue ACL
Plain body, contents on front
Quality beverages, serve cold
The Rose Beverage Co.
Illinois Glass Co.
1966

Virginia Dare Beverages—West Barrington, RI?
—need proof

Warwick Club, Club Soda—W. Warwick, RI (12 w. colors) (uncommon)
WC-1
Clear, 7oz., red, white, and dark blue ACL
It sings in the glass slogan
Stippled body (also plain body)
Warwick Club Ginger Ale Co., Inc.
Anchor Hocking Glass Co.
1953 stippled, 1961 plain

WC-2
Clear, 7oz., red, white, and dark blue ACL
It sings in the glass slogan
Stippled body
A product of the…
Warwick Club Ginger Ale Co., Inc.
Glenshaw Glass Co.
1963?

WC-3
Clear, 7oz., red, white, and dark blue ACL
It sings in the glass slogan
Stippled body
Composed of carbonated water, lithium salts
Warwick Club Ginger Ale Co., Inc.
Anchor Hocking Glass Co.
1949

Warwick Club Beverages—W. Warwick, RI (common)
WC-4
Clear, green, 7oz., red, white, and yellow ACL
Arch design on shoulder and heel
It sings in the glass slogan
Back writing on four lines
7oz. on back
Anchor Hocking Glass Co.
1954, 1958 (clear),
Glenshaw Glass Co.
1963 (green), 1948 (clear?)

WC-5
Clear, 7oz., red, white, and yellow ACL
Arch design on shoulder and heel
It sings in the glass slogan
Back writing on five lines
Contents 7 fl. Oz. on back
Owens Illinois Glass Co.
1948

WC-6
Clear, Green, 7oz., red, white, and yellow ACL
Arch design on shoulder and heel
It sings in the glass slogan
Back writing on five lines
Contents 7 fluid ozs. on back
Anchor Hocking Glass Co.
1955, 1967 clear, 1956, 1964 green

WC-7
Clear, 7oz., red, white, and yellow ACL
Arch design on shoulder and heel
It sings in the glass slogan
7oz. on front
Glenshaw Glass Co.
1967

WC-8
Clear, 7 oz., red, white, and yellow ACL
Swirled rib pattern on shoulder and heel
It sings in the glass slogan
Three lines on back
Glenshaw Glass Co.
1969

WC-9
Clear, green, 7oz., red, white, and yellow ACL
Plain bottle, no design
It sings in the glass slogan
Glenshaw Glass Co.
1970, 1971

Wellington Club Beverages—Providence, RI (uncommon, green scarce)
WL-1
Clear, green, 28oz., red and white ACL
House on front, Lobello Spring
Phone Dexter 0130
Lobello Spring Water and Soda Co.
Reed Glass Co.
1946 (green), 1947

WL-2
Clear, quart, red and white ACL
House on front, Lobello Spring
Phone Dexter 1-0130

Lobello Spring Water and Soda Co.
Reed Glass Co.
1955

WL-3
Clear, 8oz., red and white ACL
House on front
Phone 1-0130
Lobello Spring Water & Soda Co.
Reed Glass Co.
1953

WL-4
Clear, 8oz., red and white ACL
House on front
Phone 0130
Lobello Spring Water & Soda Co.
Reed Glass Co.
1947

Westerly Club Beverages, Westerly, RI (rare)
WE-1
Clear, 12oz., red and white ACL
Havens Bottling Works
Phone 2147
Havens Bottling Westerly, R.I. embossed on base
Stippled body, rings on shoulder
Reed Glass Co.
1941, 45

WE-2
Green, 1pt. 12 fld. Ozs., red and white ACL
Havens Bottling Works
Phone 2147
plain body
Reed Glass Co.
1942?

WE-3
Clear, 1pt. 12 fld. Ozs., red and white ACL
Havens Bottling Works
Phone 2147
Registered embossed on base
plain body
Reed Glass Co.
1947

Xtra—West Barrington, RI (scarce)
XR-1
Clear, 12oz., red and white ACL
Deep Rock Inc.
Embossed waist, Xtra Good, Large, Delicious below shoulder
Owens Illinois Glass Co.
1941

XR-2
Clear, 12oz., red and white ACL
Deep Rock Inc.
Embossed waist, Xtra Good, Large, Delicious below shoulder
Reg. U.S. Pat. Off below Xtra
Owens Illinois Glass Co.
1941

Yacht Club Beverages—Centerdale, RI (15) (common, 2-color versions uncommon)
YC-1
Clear, oz., red and white ACL
Very likely to exist, find one!

YC-2
Clear, 7.5oz., white and green ACL
Screen lattice design in bands on shoulder and heel
Sailboat on front, serve cold on shoulder
Yacht Club Bottling Works
Owens Illinois Glass Co.
1944, 47, 1954

YC-3
Clear, 12 oz., white and green ACL
Screen lattice design in bands on shoulder and heel, two rings around neck
Sailboat on front
Yacht Club Bottling Works
Owens Illinois Glass Co.
1941

YC-4
Clear, 28 fl. Oz., white and green ACL
Screen lattice design in bands on shoulder and heel
Serve cold on shoulder
Yacht Club Bottling Works
Owens Illinois Glass Co.
1942

YC-5
Clear, green, 7.5oz., white ACL
Screen lattice design in bands on shoulder and heel
Serve cold on shoulder
Yacht Club Bottling Works
Illinois Glass Co.
1963 (green)

YC-6
Clear, 7.5 oz., white ACL
Screen lattice design in bands on shoulder and heel
Deposit bottle on shoulder, 7-1/2 oz. on front

Yacht Club Bottling Works, with address
Illinois Glass Co.
1966

YC-7
Clear, 8oz., white ACL
Entire body is stippled
Deposit bottle on shoulder, 8oz. on front
Yacht Club Bottling Works, with address
Thatcher Glass Co.
1967

YC-8
Clear, 12oz., white ACL
Screen lattice design in bands on shoulder and heel
May be white and green ACL w/ green worn off?

YC-9
Clear, 12oz., white ACL
Plain bottle, ring at shoulder/neckline
Serve cold on neck
Yacht Club Bottling Works, no address
Illinois Glass Co.
1966

YC-10
Clear, Green, 28oz., white ACL
Screen lattice design in bands on shoulder and heel
Serve cold on shoulder
Yacht Club Bottling Works, no address
Owens Illinois Glass Co.
1946 (green), 1966 (clear)

YC-11
Clear, 28oz., white ACL
Screen lattice design in bands on shoulder and heel
Deposit Bottle on shoulder
Yacht Club Bottling Works, with address
Illinois Glass Co,
1968

YC-12
Clear, Green, quart, white ACL
Lightly stippled body
Yacht Club Bottling Works

YC-13
Green, 28oz., white ACL
Plain bottle, deposit bottle on neck

Yacht Club Bottling Works, with address
Illinois Glass Co.
1971

Yankee Beverages—Providence, RI
(uncommon)

YA-1
Clear, 12oz., blue and white ACL
Yankee hat on front, art deco ribs
Liberty Club S.W. Co. Providence, RI embossed on base
Providence, RI on base only
Glenshaw Glass Co.
M on lip- 1941

YA-2
Clear, 12oz., blue and white ACL
Yankee hat on front, art deco ribs
Liberty Club Soda Water Co.
Glenshaw Glass Co.
1953

AK-1 Better Beverages var green   **AK-1** back   **AK-1** Better Beverages var clear   **AK-2** Beta Beverages var

AK-2 back   **AK-3** back   **AK-4** Beta Beverages   **AK-4** back

AK-4 base   **AT-1** Alkalize 7oz var   **AT-1** back   **AT-1** base

AT-2 Alkalize 6½oz var   **AT-2** back   **AK-3** Refresh var   **AK-3** back

   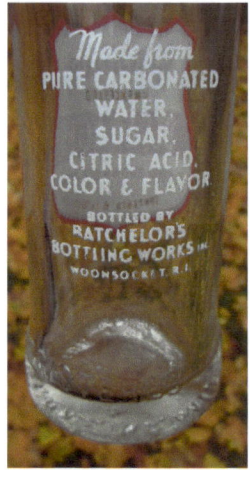

BA-1   **BA-1** back   **BA-2**   **BA-2** back

BA-2 base   **BA-3**   **BA-3** back   **BA-4** back

BA-5 **BA-5** back **BA-6** **BA-6** back

BA-7 **BA-7** back **BA-8** **BA-8** back

BA-8 base **BA-8** clear **BA-9** white neck label **BA-10**

49

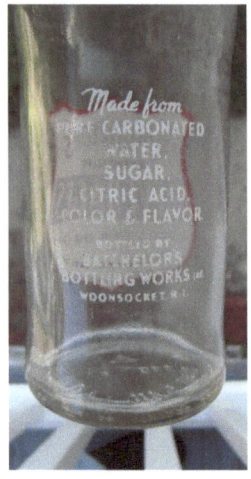   

BA-10 back　　　**BA-11**　　　**BA-11** back　　　**BA-12**

BA-12 back　　　**BA-12** clear　　　**BA-13**　　　**BA-13** back

BA-14　　　**BA-14** back　　　**BA-15**　　　**BA-15** back

BA-16   **BA-16** back   **BA-17**   **BA-17** back

BC-1   **BC-1** back   **BC-2** Blue Ribbon   **BC-2** back

BC-2 clear   **BC-3**   **BC-3** back   **BC-3** green

51

BC-4 Blue Ribbon   **BC-4** back   **BC-5**   **BC-5** back

BC-6 Blue Ribbon   **BC-6** back   **BC-7** Blue Ribbon   **BC-7** back

   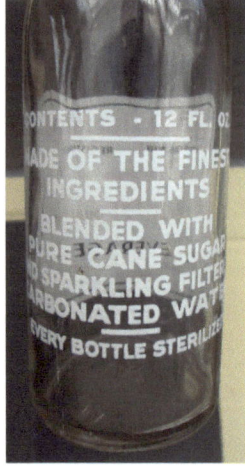

BC-8 Blue Ribbon   **BC-8** back   **BC-9**   **BC-9** back

BC-10

BC-10 back

BC-10 clear

BC-12

BC-12 back

BC-13

BC-14

BC-14 back

BC-15

BC-15 back

BC-16

BC-16 back

BL-1

BL-1 back

BR-1

BR-2

BR-2 back

BR-3

BR-3 back

BR-4

BR-5

BR-5 back

BR-7

BR-7 back

BR-8   **BR-8** back   **BR-9**   **BR-9** back

BR-10   **BR-10** back   **BR-10** clear   **BR-11**

BR-11 back   **BS-1**   **BS-1** close   **BS-1** back

55

CC-1 Newport 10oz

CC-1 base

CC-2 Newport 12oz

CC-2 close up

CC-2 base

CC-3 Newport 16oz

CC-3 close up

CC-4 Peace Dale 6½oz

CC-4 base

CC-5

CC-5 close up

CC-5 base

CC-6 Peace Dale 12oz   **CC-7** Peace Dale 16oz   **CC-7** close up   **CC-8** Providence 6½oz.

CC-8 base   **CC-9** Providence 10oz.   **CC-10** 10oz. variant   **CC-10** close up

CC-11 money back var   **CC-12** 16oz. Providence   **CC-13** 26oz. Providence   **CC-13** close up

CC-14 26oz variant

CC-14 close up

CD-1

CD-1 back

CH-1

CH-1 back

CL-2

CL-2 back

CL-2 shoulder

CL-3

CL-3 back

CL-3 shoulder

CL-4

CL-4 back

CL-5

CL-5 back

CL-6

CL-6 close

CL-6 back

CL-7

CL-7 back

CL-8

CL-8 back

CL-9

CL-9 back

CN-1

CN-1 back

CN-2

CN-2 back

CN-3

CN-3 back

CN-3 clear

CT-1

CT-1 back

CT-2

CT-2 back

 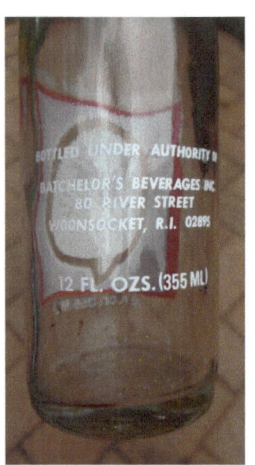  

DM-1   **DM-1** back   **DR-1**   **DR-1** clear

DR-1 base   **DR-2**   **DR-2** back   **DR-2** clear

DR-2 back   **DS-1**   **DS-1** back   **DS-2**

DS-2 back

DS-2 clear

DS-3

DS-3 back

DV-1

DV-1 back

DV-2

DV-2 back

DX-1

DX-1 back

DX-2

DX-2 back

DX-2 clear   **DX-3**   **DX-3** back   **DX-4**

DX-4 back   **DX-4** clear   **DY-1**   **DY-1** close

DY-1 clear   **DY-2**   **DY-2** back   **DY-3**

DY-3 back   **EA-1**   **EA-1** back   **EA-2**

EA-2 back   **EC-1**   **EC-1** back   **EM-1**

EM-1 back   **EM-2**   **EM-2** back   **EM-3**

  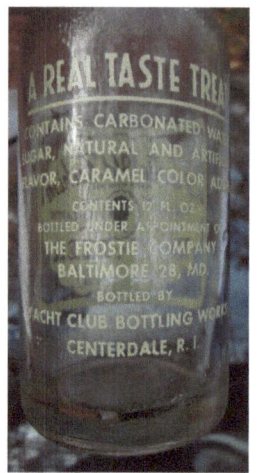 

EM-3 back   **FR-1**   **FR-1** back   **FY-1**

FY-1 back   **GC-1**   **GC-1** back   **GC-2**

GC-2 back   **GC-3** green   **GC-3** back   **GC-3** clear

GR-1   **GR-1** back   **GR-2**   **GR-2** back

GS-1   **GS-1** back   **GS-2**   **GS-2** back

HC-1   **HC-1** back   **HC-2**   **HC-2** back

67

HC-3

HC-3 back

HC-4

HC-4 back

HC-5

HC-5 back

HC-6

HC-6 back

HC-7

HC-7 clear

HC-7 back

HC-8

 **HC-8** back

 **HC-8** clear

 **HC-9**

 **HC-9** back

 **HC-10**

 **HC-10** back

 **HC-10** clear

 **HC-11**

 **HC-11** back

 **HC-11** clear

 **HC-12**

 **HC-12** back

HC-12 clear **HE-1** **HE-1** back **ID-1**

ID-1 back **ID-2** **ID-2** back **KB-1**

KB-2 **KR-1** **KR-1** back **LA-1**

   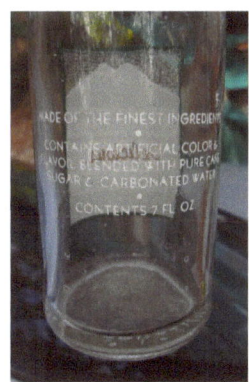

LA-1 back   **LA-1** clear   **LA-2**   **LA-2** back

LC-1   **LC-1** back   **LC-1** clear   **LC-1** color variant

LC-2   **LC-2** back   **LC-3**   **LC-3** back

LG-1   **LG-1** back   **LG-2**   **LG-2** back

LU-1   **LU-1** back   **MA-1**   **MA-1** back

 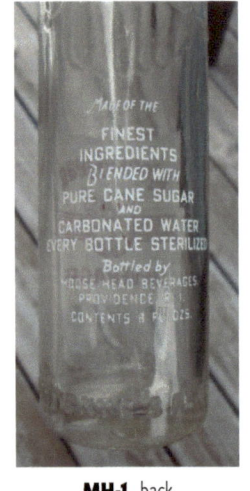  

MH-1   **MH-1** back   **MH-2**   **MH-2** back

MH-3   **MH-3** back   **MH-3** green   **MH-4**

MI-1   **MI-1** back   **MI-2**   **MI-2** back

MI-3   **MI-3** back   **MI-4**   **MI-4** back

73

MI-5

MI-5 back

MI-6

MI-6 back

MN-1

MN-1 close

MN-2

MN-2 back

MN-2 clear

MN-3

MN-3 back

MN-4

MN-5  **MN-5** close **MN-6** **MN-6** back

MN-6 green  **MN-7** **MN-7** back **MN-7** clear

MN-9  **MN-9** back **MN-10** **MN-10** back

75

MN-10 clear

MR-1

MR-1 back

NC-1

NC-1 back

NC-1 clear

NE-1

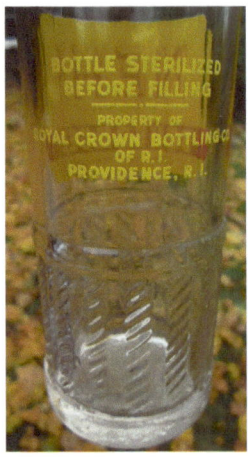
NE-1 back

NU-1

NU-1 back

NU-2

NU-2 back

 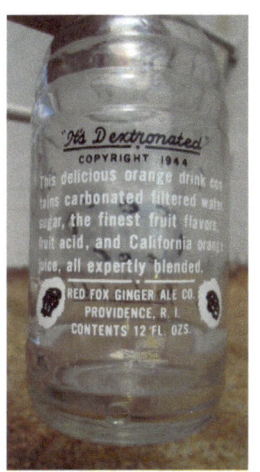  

NU-3   **NU-3** back   **OC-1**   **OC-1** back

OC-2   **OC-2** back   **OC-3**   **OC-3** back (embossed registered)

OC-4   **OC-4** back   **OC-5**   **OC-5** back

OC-6   **OC-6** back   **OC-7**   **OC-7** back

OC-8   **OC-8** back   **OC-10**   **OC-10** back

OC-11   **OE-1**   **OE-1** back   **PC-1** double dot on neck

PC-1 back　　**PC-2** single dot on neck　　**PC-2** back　　**PC-3**

PC-3 back　　**PC-4** double dot　　**PC-4** back　　**PC-5**

PC-5 back　　**PC-6** of RI　　**PC-6** back　　**PC-7**

PC-7 back　　　**PC-8** of RI　　　**PC-8** back　　　**PC-9**

PC-9 back　　　**PC-10**　　　**PC-10** back　　　**PC-10** back shoulder

RC-1　　　**RC-1** back　　　**RC-2**　　　**RC-2** back

RF-1   **RF-1** back   **RF-1** clear   **RF-2**

RF-2 back   **RF-2** clear   **RF-3**   **RF-3** back

RF-4   **RF-4** back   **RF-5**   **RF-5** back

RO-1 **RO-1** back **RO-1** clear **RO-2**

RO-2 back **RO-2** green **RO-3** parentheses around pint **RO-3** back

 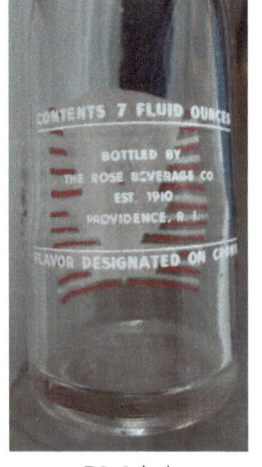  

RO-4 **RO-4** back **RO-4** green **RO-5**

RO-5 back

RR-1

RR-1 back

RR-2

RR-2 back

RZ-1

RZ-1 back

RZ-1 clear

RZ-2

RZ-2 back

RZ-3

RZ-3 back

83

RZ-4   **RZ-4** back   **RZ-4** clear   **SB-1**

SB-1 back   **SB-2**   **SB-2** arched   **SB-3** red

SB-3 back   **SC-1**   **SC-1** back   **SC-2**

SC-2 back **SE-1** **SE-1** back **SE-2**

SE-2 back **SH-1** **SH-1** back **SH-2**

SH-2 back **SH-3** hollow headdress **SI-1** **SI-1** close

SI-2   **SI-2** back   **SK-1**   **SK-1** back

SP-1   **SP-1** close   **SP-2**   **SP-2** back

SP-3   **SP-3** back   **SP-4**   **SP-4** back

SQ-1

SQ-1 back

SQ-2

SQ-2 back

ST-2

ST-2 back

ST-3

ST-3 back

SU-1

SU-1 back

SU-2

SU-2 back

87

SU-3 **SU-3** back **SU-4** substituted **SU-5**

SU-5 back **SU-6** **SU-6** back **SU-7**

SU-7 back **SU-8** **SU-8** back **SU-9**

SU-9 back **SW-1** **SW-1** back **SW-2**

SW-2 back **SW-3** **SW-3** back **TA-1** 6.5 oz.

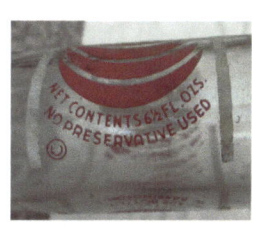

TA-1 sides **TA-2** 6.5 oz. **TA-2** sides **TA-3** 6.5 oz.

TA-4 7 oz.   **TA-4** sides OZ   **TA-5** 7 oz.   **TA-5** sides OZS

 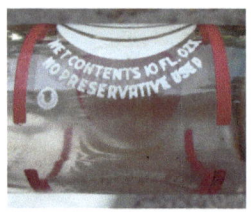    

TA-6 King Size 10 oz.   **TA-6** sides   **TA-7** King Size ver2   **TA-7** sides

TA-8 10 oz.   **TA-8** shoulder   **TA-9** 10 oz.   **TA-9** shoulder

TW-2 back   **VD-1**   **VD-1** back   **VD-2**

 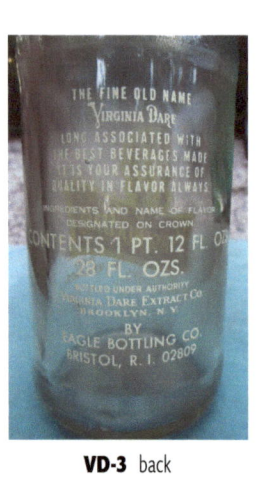  

VD-3   **VD-3** back   **VD-4**   **VD-4** back

VD-5   **VD-5** back   **VD-8**   **VD-8** back

VD-9   **VD-9** back   **VD-9** clear   **VD-10**

VD-10 back   **VD-11**   **VD-11** back   **VD-12**

VD-12 back   **VD-13**   **VD-13** back   **VD-13** green

93

VD-14

VD-14 back

VD-15

VD-15 back

WC-1

WC-1 back

WC-1 stippled body

WC-2

WC-2 back

WC-3

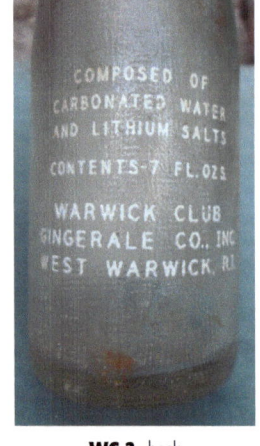
WC-3 back

WC-4

   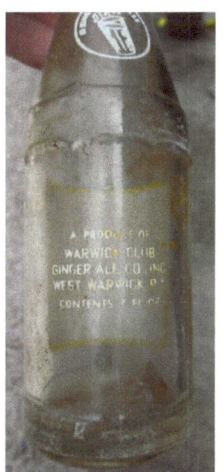

WC-4 back   **WC-4** clear   **WC-5**   **WC-5** back FL OZ

 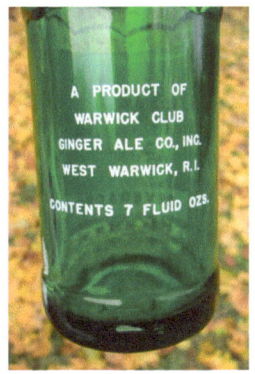  

WC-6   **WC-6** back FLUID   **WC-6** clear   **WC-7**

WC-7 back   **WC-8**   **WC-8** back   **WC-9**

WC-9 back   **WC-9** clear   **WE-1**   **WE-1** back

WE-1 clear   **WE-2**   **WE-2** back   **WE-3**

WE-3 back   **WL-1**   **WL-1** back   **WL-1** clear

WL-2

WL-2 back

WL-3

WL-3 back

WL-4

WL-4 back

XR-1

XR-1 close

XR-2

XR-2 close

YA-1

YA-1 back

97

   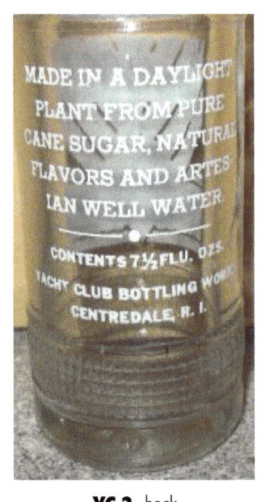

YA-2 **YA-2** back **YC-2** **YC-2** back

   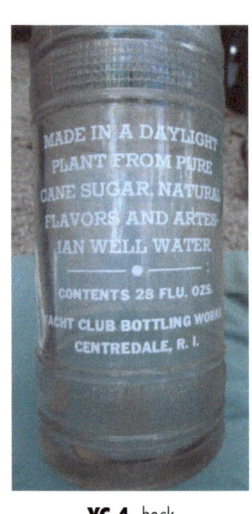

YC-3 **YC-3** back **YC-4** **YC-4** back

YC-5 Serve cold **YC-5** back **YC-5** clear **YC-6** Deposit bottle

 **YC-6** back

 **YC-7**

 **YC-7** back

 **YC-9**

 **YC-9** back

 **YC-10** Serve cold

 **YC-10** back

 **YC-10** clear

 **YC-11** Deposit bottle

 **YC-11** back

 **YC-13**

 **YC-13** back

99

www.ingramcontent.com/pod-product-compliance
Lightning Source LLC
Chambersburg PA
CBHW042016150426
43197CB00002B/48